MIDLAND COUNTIES

WALKS FOR MOTORISTS

Richard Shurey

30 Walks with sketch maps

COUNTRYSIDE BOOKS

NEWBURY, BERKSHIRE

First Published 1982
by Frederick Warne Ltd.
© Richard Shurey 1982

This completely revised and updated edition
published 1990
Reprinted 1992
© Richard Shurey, 1992

COUNTRYSIDE BOOKS
3, Catherine Road,
Newbury, Berkshire

ISBN 1 85306 105 0

Sketch maps by the author

Cover photograph taken from
the British Camp, Malvern
by Andy Williams

Produced through MRM Associates Ltd., Reading
Printed by J. W. Arrowsmith Ltd., Bristol

Contents

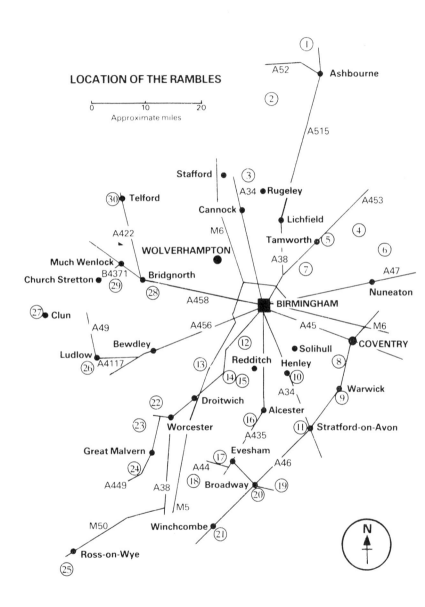

LOCATION OF THE RAMBLES

Introduction

The Midland Counties have some of the most varied and lovely countryside in the land. To see this countryside from a car is impossible — the only way is to venture along rights of way footpaths to the quiet unhurried places.

Apart from the sheer joy of seeing attractive landscapes and finding pretty villages, there is the therapeutic benefits of rambling as an antidote to the hectic pressures of life today. Visit the countryside on a day in early spring and see the first crocus or daffodil emerging, or ramble along a woodland track dappled in autumnal tints, kicking up coppered leaves.

Many pastimes require expensive equipment and detailed costly instruction — not so with walking. Ordinary stout footwear, everyday clothing suitable for the prevailing climatic conditions are the necessities and the open air world is yours for exploring. You will enjoy the experience — and good health will be a gigantic free bonus.

Whether you travel alone or with companions is a matter of choice — many folk love the solitude of walking alone with Nature, setting their own pace to linger and wander where they will. Others find that this is one occasion when they have time to talk and communicate in today's busy world. I have often recommended lonely people to join a rambling club — it is impossible to walk in silence even if it is only idle chat about the weather or the lovely view.

Several of the walks mention Youth Hostels which are open to all members (of any age) of the Youth Hostels Association. It is possible to join at the hostels but prior booking is advisable. More details can be obtained from The Youth Hostels Association, Trevelyan House, St. Albans, Herts AL1 2DY.

I have had great pleasure in preparing these walks. I hope that the reader will go out and enjoy them too.

Richard Shurey
May 1990

The following symbols appear at the beginning of each walk and give a quick guide to the facilities available on that particular route.

 Opening times of castles, museums, gardens and other places of interest, together with admission fees where appropriate

 Availability of refreshments en route — ices, teas etc.

 Inns along the route or within short detour from main walk

 Ordnance Survey map of the particular area should you wish to use one in addition to the sketch map

 The best place to park at the start of the walk

 Youth hostel

 The beginning of the walk

DOVE DALE

WALK 1

4 miles (6.5 km)

The poet Tennyson called the valley of the little River Dove 'one of the most unique and delicious places in the land'. One must admit that today, compared with when the poet came to these parts, the dale can attract a lot of visitors. But the place is still most attractive at all seasons of the year.

Izaak Walton made the Dove Dale popular when he published his *Compleat Angler* in 1653. His friend, Charles Cotton, was another poet and he composed for the book a treatise on fly fishing. Further upstream on this ramble the waters are well weeded, giving cover for the fish. Stop awhile and you will probably see a cautious plump fish emerge!

The limestone cliffs have been dissected by the frosts of time and romantic names have been given to the weird shapes — on this walk we pass by Ilam Rock, Lion's Head Rock and the lofty Tissington Spires. The limestone is relatively soft and dissolves — at Dove Holes we can see that once the river was much higher up the gorge than today — the caves have been left 'dry' and are now the welcome home for bats.

Thorpe Cloud overlooks the start of the walk — fossil hunters come here to look for the shapes of animals who lived, it is estimated, 320 million years ago.

I have indicated the route as going to Dove Holes then returning by the river directly to the starting place. After Dove Holes the gorge opens out and the way is more pastoral. If you want the longer walk the path does continue by the waterside through 'squeeze' stiles to Milldale. This place — a huddle of stone cottages — is beloved by the walker and the artist. There is also a charming café overlooking the river.

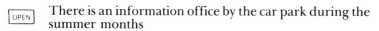

OPEN	There is an information office by the car park during the summer months
	Refreshment kiosk by car park, café in Milldale
	Ordnance Survey 1:50,000 series, no 119
P	Car park off the Thorpe to Ilam road
	Youth hostel in Ilam

By the car park the river has cut deeply into the limestone. Go over the footbridge which gives access to the pathway which hugs the riverside. High to the right is the peak of Thorpe Cloud where the Romans had a strategic settlement.

By a bend in the river children can have fun leaping the stepping stones. Here the character of the water changes, no longer tumbling and speeding, and the river becomes wide and placid. There are glades of beech and the rowan berries are vivid in the autumn months; the clear water goes over gentle falls. On the rocky crags here you may see mountaineers practising their sport with ropes and crampons to give a grip on the rocks.

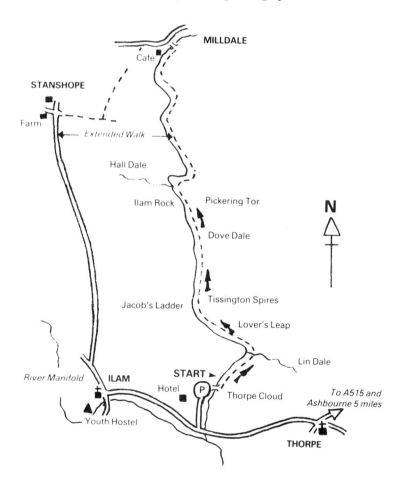

Soon look for a bold track leaving the river by climbing to the right. Take care, you romantics, for here is lover's leap. From the heights we can hear but not see the river which is far, far below in the trees. Now keep straight ahead to descend again to the water's edge. The river here is a most haunting green — especially if the sunlight is filtered onto it through the trees.

We pass by tall rock formations, all of which have names — Tissington Spires, the Apostle Rocks and the twin tower pinnacles of Ilam Rock and Pickering Tor. Do not go over the bridge but continue to the great caves of Dove Holes.

On the opposite bank are the trees of Hunt Wood alongside Hall Dale — vast woodlands. Because of their height and inaccessibility they have been allowed to grow and develop without man's disturbance. Unless you are going on to Milldale, retrace your steps along the way of the outward journey back to the car park.

THE FUN PLACE OF ALTON TOWERS

WALK 2

7 miles (11 km)

The great mansion of Alton Towers was once the home of the Talbots — earls of Shrewsbury. It was Charles, the fifteenth earl, who created the magnificent gardens in 1814 by bringing to the rugged North Staffordshire countryside labourers and skilled workers in many trades to excavate the lakes and pools with their numerous fountains, to lay out the gardens and terraces and build all the architectural wonders.

It was John, who followed the gardener, Charles, who completed the house, adding halls, galleries and fortifications and naming it Alton Towers. It was said to have been the biggest private house in Europe.

The Talbots established themselves in a castle on a cliff on the southern banks of the River Churnet at the end of the Hundred Years War. Charles looked across the gorge-like valley to a site of a pre-historic fort and decreed that 'a stately pleasure dome' be erected. Over the vast estate of 600 acres of wilderness he planned his grand design.

It remained the home of the Talbots until 1924, when the estate was sold and the huge battlemented house began to fall into ruin. It was used by the Army during World War II as an Officer Cadet Training Unit; by the end of the war the place was in a dilapidated state.

In 1952, the grounds were reopened to the public and amusements and places of fun gradually added. Today, besides the magnificent buildings, we can enjoy the amusement park and fairground, aerial cable cars, scenic railway, a giant model railway, donkey rides and boating and paddling pools — so choose a fine day!

OPEN Alton Towers is open daily from Good Friday to the first weekend in October

Cafés and restaurants at Alton Towers

Inns in Denstone and Alton

Ordnance Survey 1:50,000 series, no 128

P Quiet street, Denstone

There are two starts from Denstone. To reduce the length of the walk, keep along the B5032 from Denstone village for a little over a mile. For the longer route from the centre of the village and the Tavern Inn, go along the no through road signposted to Denstone College.

We soon leave the houses behind and there is a stile and footpath finger post pointing the way to Denstone College. Keep by the line of hawthorn bushes to climb a stile in the corner of a field. Go diagonally over the next field. To the right of a white house is a stile leading to a vehicle way. There are now fine views over the vale.

Go a step or two to the left to a gap and to the playing fields of Denstone College — this public school was founded a little over a hundred years ago. Cut straight across the grass, keeping just to the left of the chapel. Keep ahead past the buildings, then turn right through a squeeze stile. Walk in front of the college by the memorial to students who died in the wars. In the corner of the field is a metal gate; a step or so along a cinder track is a stile into a meadow.

Keep ahead now (hedge on right). The stile here is a huge lump of sandstone; more stiles are waymarked. In sheep lands walk through a metal gate — the next arrow can be seen on an oak tree. Take care by a dried-up pool to keep on the same heading; there are two stiles concealed in the bushes.

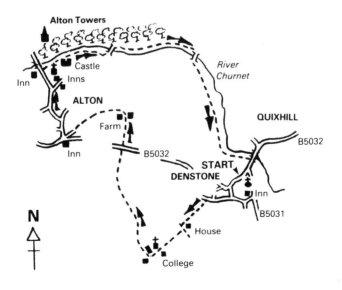

11

We come to the B5032 to join the shorter route. Cross straight over to the drive of Holbrook Farm. Turn left by the farm along an ancient road — Saltersford Lane. This was one of England's network of salt-ways when the mineral was such an important preservative.

At a road junction turn along the way to the right (signposted to Alton). Along Lime Kiln Lane we come to the round lock-up of days past and the romantic grandeur of Alton. This part of the Churnet gorge is called the 'Staffordshire Rhineland'. Cross the river — there is then a steep climb along the road to the entrance to the fun-land of Alton Towers.

Retrace your steps to the river. Opposite the inn a pathway starts. Go along a farm drive so the castle ramparts are on the right and river on the left. Just before a stone cottage climb a stile on the left. This way leads to a riverside path and then a railed bridge to cross the water.

Continue to the way the trains once ran and turn right along the clinker path. The sides of the vale are steep and clad in bracken. At a road bridge join the B5032 and turn right to Denstone.

SHUGBOROUGH HALL AND CANNOCK CHASE

WALK 3

4½ or 7 miles (7 or 11 km)

One of our most famous admirals was Anson, and many warships over the centuries have been named HMS Anson. On this walk we visit his home, Shugborough Hall; and what a home it is!

Shugborough Hall is now owned by the National Trust and administered by the Staffordshire County Council. There are still private apartments — the county home of the Earl of Lichfield, cousin of the Queen and a noted photographer.

The Staffordshire County Museum is now housed in the old stables adjacent to the hall. There are some fascinating things to see — we can have a glimpse of buildings of the past such as a tailor's shop, brewhouse and coach houses.

In the park of Shugborough keep your eyes peeled for the eighteenth-century follies designed by James Stuart. Based on Greek classical designs, the triumphal arch is especially impressive. The farm on the estate is now an agricultural museum, including rare and historic breeds of livestock.

We also walk over part of the vast heathlands of Cannock Chase. This was a royal forest which is rather surprising, as usually a 'chase' was the term for woodland owned by a commoner.

Henry II often hunted on the Chase staying at Radmore Lodge and you may be lucky enough to see a herd of the fallow deer that roam the 28 square miles of uplands.

OPEN Shugborough Hall is open daily from March to Christmas.
Admission charges: Museum — £2.00 adults £1.50 children. *Farm* — £2.00 adults £1.50 children. *Hall* — £2.00 adults £1.50 children. Combined ticket — £5.00 adults £3.00 children. Family ticket £10.00

Cafés in Shugborough and Milford Common

Inns in Milford and Great Haywood

Ordnance Survey 1:50,000 series, no 127

P Car park at Milford Common

From Milford Common on the A513, take the lane by the gates of Shugborough — signposted to Tixall. There are then three bridges over the main railway, the River Trent and an 'up and downer' across a canal.

The quiet way leads to a junction; bear right by a stone plinth and seat at the hamlet of Tixall. The monument has marked this spot since 1776. There is a cottage or two with neat gardens and the little church of John the Baptist (built 1849).

Around some bends (take care) you can see the towered Tudor Gatehouse of Ingestre. The fine Georgian mansion was pulled down in 1927. To this place, in 1586, Mary Queen of Scots was lured by a trick and was imprisoned in the great house for seventeen days.

By Tixall Farm is the old six-sided toll house. Go through the nearby gate — the path is signed. A farm vehicle way goes through lush pastures not far from the canal embankment. Through a gate by a house we regain the lane and turn right. On a river bridge glance to the right where an arched aqueduct takes the canal over the river.

We go by the old mill of Haywood Mill to a junction and proceed to the right. There is the rather unusual tower of a Catholic church. Keep ahead by the inn and post office to walk under the railway arches. We now go over Essex Bridge — said to be the longest pack-horse bridge in England. It once had 40 arches (now it has 14) and was built by the Earl of Essex in the seventeenth century. This way over the canal leads to Shugborough Hall and the route can be shortened by walking along the drive back to Milford.

For a longer route retrace your steps to the canal. Walk southwards along the towing path. At bridge no 72 (we are now at Little Haywood) leave the waterway and walk along the lane under the railway. There is the old cobbled bridge 'erected by public subscription but mainly through the liberality of Joseph Weetman Esq. in the year 1887–8'.

At the A513 cross over and walk along the vehicle track leading to Seven Springs. At the end of a car park bear right to go by a vehicle barrier. After 300 yards, there is a division of ways. We swing right past another barrier and a notice, 'no vehicles', with a sign telling us that this area is of 'special scientific interest where wildlife and plants have legal protection'.

Ignore the bold turning — we keep ahead along a sandy way edged with bracken. There are now other turnings but our way is still straight ahead with dense pine plantations away to your right. We keep by a 'no public access' stretch of woodlands (on right side) and descend to stepping-stones. Here a clear brook

14

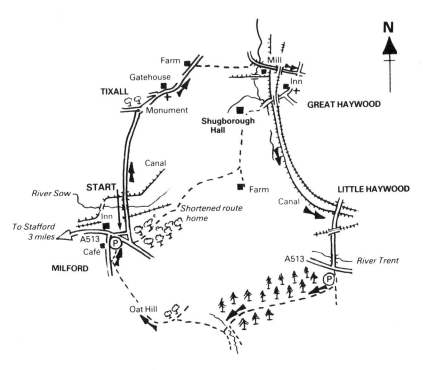

meanders through a glade and children will delight in chasing through the water.

Over the stream take the wide track going right. After ¾ mile there is a car park area and a steep hill ahead. Turn left so the hill is on your right. The wide track swings right and climbs a little incline where there is a junction of ways. Keep on the same heading along a V-shaped valley, the banks of which are covered with gorse.

We reach a road by an old folks' rest home. Immediately leave the road again to go by a 'no parking' sign. This way leads to Milford Common.

15

WE'RE GOING TO THE ZOO

WALK 4

4½ miles (7 km)

At Twycross, in the north-west corner of Leicestershire, there is a marvellous zoo in the heart of the countryside. The zoo was registered as a charity in 1972 with very enlightened aims — 'To educate the public in a greater knowledge of all wild life and conservation; to promote and encourage the study of zoology and its kindred sciences; to provide and assist in the provision and facilities for recreation and leisure time occupations in the interest of social welfare'.

The zoo also aims to increase the number of animals, especially species in danger of extinction, by controlled breeding. The zoo started in 1950 as a private collection of animals at Hints in Staffordshire. When the popularity of the collection increased, larger premises were sought and the zoo was moved to the grounds of a large house at Twycross in 1963. It now covers 50 acres of parkland.

Besides the enormous range of large animals and exotic birds there are many other attractions. Special mention should be given to the Pets Corner (where there are children's favourites like calves, piglets, guinea pigs, rabbits, talking macaws and parrots), the miniature railway and the Chimps Tea Party (made famous on television by a well-known brand of tea!).

I like Twycross — the charges are reasonable and there are several thoughtful ideas such as special facilities for physically handicapped children, encouragement for the mentally retarded, educational programmes for school parties, children-only menus and massive urns of orange squash for thirsty youngsters!

The walk to the zoo starts at the little village of Austrey. There is an old cross here — perhaps built in the fifteeenth century. The church with a spire is a couple of hundred years older and there is a picturesque thatched inn.

 The *zoo* is open daily from 10.00 a.m. *Admission* — adults £3.00, children £1.50 and senior citizens £2.00 (good reductions for parties and schools) *Note:* No dogs allowed

 Cafeterias and tea bar at the zoo

16

🍺 Inn in Austrey

📚 Ordnance Survey 1:50,000 series, no 140

P By church at Austrey

Austrey is like many villages where there is an old 'core' with the rapid addition of new houses in recent years. From the cross in Church Lane turn left.

Opposite the post office and by a house called 'Farthings' a pathway starts. Climb a stile next to a gate which lies back off the road. Continue to the left over the stile, keeping by the back gardens of houses. By a new gate 'dog-leg' a yard or so right then regain the old heading. Keep ahead across a pasture to go through a metal gate. Still on the same bearing there is a field where cows graze. Aiming just to the right of an estate house, you will come to a step stile.

Cross a farm drive to another stile. Now cut almost diagonally across the meadow. At the far side of an off-white house, there is a kissing gate onto a lane. (If this gate will not open, use the field gate.)

Turn right along Appleby Hill. After about ¾ mile (just past the drive of Hill Farm) there is a horse shoe bridleway sign on the right. Nearby, is a thing that resembles a space-rocket made of Meccano. Actually it is a Post Office telecommunications aerial!

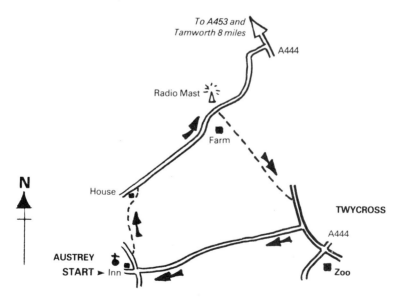

Go through a gate and along a vehicle track. Keep to the right of a concrete water tower and walk through another gate to a field which often grows barley for beer.

Keep by the right-hand hedge. The track is clear over flat countryside to the A444. Twycross Zoo is to the right. (Sometimes there is an entrance to the zoo from Orton Hill Road — right at the crossroads — otherwise use the main entrance on the A444.)

For a quick way back to Austrey go over the crossroads on the A444 then take the next road on the left (just over a mile to the village).

TAMWORTH TO A
WATER NATURE RESERVE

WALK 5

★

6 miles (9.5 km)

Nature is ever resourceful, taking advantage of a changing environment. To the east of Tamworth, in the valley of the River Anker, there are many acres of flooded abandoned industrial workings. Today, the water fowl have discovered that the old industrial disturbances have finished and they have made the huge man-made lakes either their permanent home or a staging post on their migrating travels. The waters are dotted with coots, seemingly oblivious of the fishermen and overhead the V-shaped formations of ducks are a magnificent sight.

Tamworth, the starting place, is steeped in history. The town was the site, from about AD 757, of one of the Saxon King Offa's opulent palaces.

Almost 200 years later Aethelflaeda (the daughter of the cake-burning King Alfred) gave instructions for a rampart to be built at the confluence of the rivers Tame and Anker. The same war lady also sited the great castle at Warwick. The Normans arrived and favoured the strategic site. They built a massive fortress which once covered the area of the present castle grounds.

There is a museum housed in the castle which contains items of historical and local interest.

 Tamworth Castle and *Museum* are open daily 10.00 a.m. – 5.00 p.m., Sundays 2.00 p.m. – 4.30 p.m. *Admission* – Adults £1.60, children 80p (free under 5)

 Cafés in Tamworth

 Inns in Tamworth and Amington

 Ordnance Survey 1:50,000 series, no 139

 Car park near Tamworth Station

 The walk starts at Tamworth railway station car park where there is a signposted footpath. Walk under the railway and just before a caravan site swing left. The path

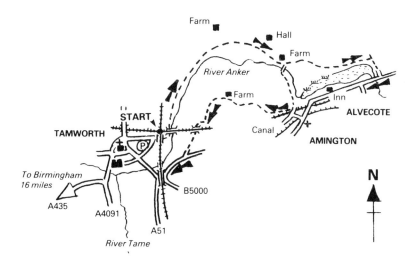

goes beside the railway embankment, then bears left to pass under the tracks again. This is a busy cross-over rail junction and few minutes pass without a train thundering through.

Under the railway swing right to join the bank of the river and keep by the tranquil waters. Still on the same heading, we go by a 'railway arch'. There is no point in waiting here to see the trains as this line was abandoned long ago and only ghost trains now run.

We come to the river again. Follow the placid reeded waters upstream. This stretch of the Anker River is fished by members of the Birmingham Angling Association — said to be the largest angling club in the land. The path goes over a wood slat bridge then wends a way above bushes and reed beds, never far from the river, to emerge in an (often) arable field.

Here, leave the river by bearing slightly left. Keep the farm and large barns well to the left. Just tip rather obsolete hedges along an undefined path.

Now, aiming for a distant white house you will come to a pole stile into a pasture. Walk just to the right of an electricity pole marker. Soon pass under the electricity wires to head towards the farm buildings of Amington Old Hall. (The 'new' Amington Hall is to the left — a rather sombre building of the last century.) Climb the fence stile under a holly bush and continue over sheep lands to the farm.

Go into the farmyard. Through the farmyard bear right to a ford and a bridge over the river. Do not cross the river but keep on the concrete 'road' bearing left by poplar trees which conceal an old moat. (If you keep ahead there is a footbridge over the river and the walk can be curtailed.)

Leave the concrete drive when it turns 90° left (to head towards distant barns). We keep ahead and climb a stile by a metal gate and walk along a wide, grassed farm track. There is a hedge on our right side, but when the boundary bears right we keep straight ahead, cutting off the end of a field, to a five-bar gate.

Adjoining the gate is a stile to climb. Still on the same heading, walk by a wire fence (on left side). To the right and left now are wide expanses of water where the wild-fowl can be silently observed.

Bear slightly left and go over a stile by a gate. Resume the old heading (wire now on right). There was once an old farm here — now all we see is some rubble. The track leads by the water's edge; there is a further stile by a field gate. Continue to a cul-de-sac lane and turn right to a T-junction.

Proceed to the right to walk over the bridges and keep ahead at a road junction (Shuttington Road). Go by the quaintly named Pretty Pig Inn. The road goes over the railway and canal to Amington. Take the first road on the right opposite a tiny church. Across the canal, bear right when the road divides to go over the railway again. Immediately, the lane turns sharp left to follow the edge of the railway.

Beyond cottages keep on the lane which twists its way past a mobile homes site and becomes a farm vehicle way. We walk at the edges of fields of cabbages and lettuces. At a junction of ways, by a metal railed gate, turn left to take the bold track (*not* by the hedge) roughly heading towards Tamworth church.

We reach rough ground — there are countless tracks but walk to the clearly seen footbridge over the railway. Do *not* go over the bridge but turn right to follow the embankment to a tunnel under the tracks. (The rough ground is a preserved ancient common).

This leads to a vehicle way at the rear of gardens. Keep walking in this direction to join an estate road which leads to a main road. This is Amington Road which leads to Tamworth.

THE BATTLE OF BOSWORTH — 1485

WALK 6

4 miles (6.5 km)

'Oh, not history', I can imagine children retorting. Often ancient sites of conflict are indeed dull — but not Bosworth Field.

Situated on the western borders of Leicestershire, Bosworth is different and exciting, for the events enacted here marked one of the most significant turning points in the history of our land.

The area has been instructively planned as a living exhibition to record — on unobtrusive plinths — the pattern of the battle. There is also an interesting museum.

Visit Bosworth and with a little imagination the fight can be relived in vivid detail; one can almost hear the twang of longbows, the clatter of sword on sword, and the cries of success and anguish, and almost smell the stench of the battle.

Richard III marched his men to Sutton Cheney, then occupied the nearby Ambion Hill early on the summer of 22 August 1485. His fickle ally, Lord Stanley, stood off on a nearby ridge waiting to see which way the fight was going.

Henry Tudor had landed in Wales and was heading south-eastwards towards London. The fateful morning was sunny and warm and Henry's troops, now camped below the slopes of Ambion Hill, were outnumbered, two to one. Henry attacked the hill with arrows and cannon and arm to arm combat followed with swords and battle-axes.

The turning point came when Henry set off to persuade the hesitant Stanley to change sides. Richard staked all with a charge on Henry himself. Seated on his white steed and with the crown of England perched over his helmet, the king galloped forward with his bodyguard, slashing right and left with his battle-axe.

He fell at Richard's Well which we visit on this ramble. Henceforth, the monarchs of our land no longer led their troops personally into the fray.

OPEN Bosworth Field Battlefield Centre is open every day from Easter to end of October

Cafés in Market Bosworth and at the Battlefield Centre

Inns in Market Bosworth and Sutton Cheney

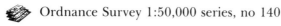 Ordnance Survey 1:50,000 series, no 140

P Car park in Market Bosworth

From the B585, a pathway is signposted (a boot emblem) at the side of a park and a restaurant.

Walk towards a lake, then keep the water just to your left. At the end of the pool, keep straight ahead. After about 100 yards enter grassland and, slightly to the left, you will see a stile and footpath sign.

Cross a pasture to another indication of direction. Over the stiles keep on, in the same direction, at the side of a field. There is a rough stile, then we veer across to the right to nudge a wood.

Proceed to a railed bridge over a brook. The next fields are sown, so walking up the incline, keep by the left-hand hedge. Follow waymarks to emerge on a lane by an inn. We go to the right to the hamlet of Sutton Cheney where there are a couple of good

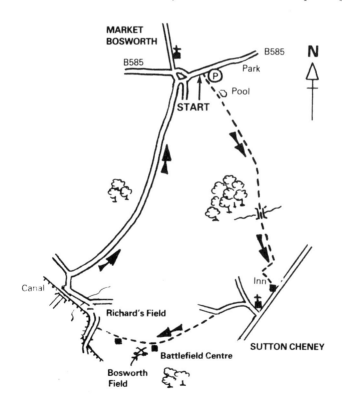

inns. The Hall with tall gables that you can now see looks Elizabethan.

At the crossroads, take the way to the right. When the lane divides, we go along the left fork. We can now see the standards fluttering on Ambion Hill. The path to Bosworth Field starts from a car park. The clear way leads to the information centre and the Battlefield Centre. The battle walk takes us to the route of the old railway line (another car park here). Part of the railway cutting has been designated as a nature reserve.

At the foot of the hill is the cairn which is Richard's Well. The Richard III Society have erected a sign to tell us that this is the spot where the king quenched his thirst and 'fell fighting gallantly in defence of his realm and his crown against the usurper, Henry Tudor'.

Continue the walk by turning along the country lane. This runs parallel to the Ashby-de-la-Zouch canal for a little way, then heads homewards to Market Bosworth.

KINGSBURY WATER PARK

WALK 7

3 miles (5 km)

This walk begins at Kingsbury. Perched on the top of a cliff above the river, alongside the church built by the Normans, is an old and crumbling structure that has traces in great stones and archways of the splendours of an Elizabethan fortified house or castle.

It has been suggested that it may have been the site of a palace of the Mercian Kings — Mercia covered a great tract of the Midlands stretching as far as the Welsh borderlands, along which Offa built his Dyke.

On the other side of the church — in Church Lane — is the School House. It is about three hundred years old — a gracious building from the days when schooling was the privilege of only the rich.

Kingsbury Country Park is situated across the River Tame. Until a year or so ago much of the area was derelict land and lakes where sand and gravel had been extracted. Now all sorts of leisure activities can be enjoyed — there is sailing and high-speed boating, water skiing and fishing. Especially for children are model-boat pools, paddling pools, adventure playgrounds with marvellous contraptions to climb and picnic places.

OPEN   Kingsbury Country Park is open every day. Admission is free for walkers

Refreshments in Kingsbury Country Park

Inns in Kingsbury

Ordnance Survey 1:50,000 series, no 139

Kingsbury

From Kingsbury churchyard, steps lead down to a footbridge over the River Tame. This area is subject to flooding and the pathway is on a causeway.

Soon to the right is the adventure playground and grassed areas where footballs can be kicked and games of cricket organized.

With so much water around and marshy areas now

25

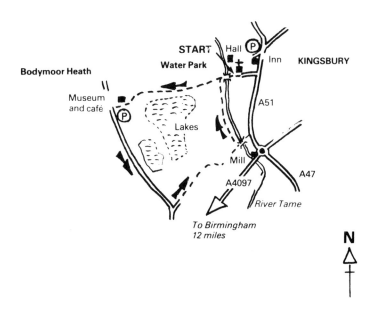

undisturbed by man, it is little surprising that large numbers of wildfowl make their home at Kingsbury.

Keep ahead to reach the old farm building where a little museum is housed. We are told here that bream, carp, roach, tench, perch and pike can be caught in the lakes (fishing licences are available for a modest fee).

A log of the migration of birds is kept and there are examples of the three hundred species of flowers which flourish in the park.

On the lane turn left, then left again after almost a mile. We are now on the old road — now only walkers come this way to Hemlingford Bridge. This was once an old fording place of the river; in 1783 a public subscription list was opened to raise funds for the building of the bridge we see today.

Over the other side of the river there has been a mill at least as far back as the Domesday survey of 1086. Now used as a garden centre it has been a gun barrel mill, sawmill, paper mill, leather mill and grain mill in its long and chequered history.

A pathway borders the river to return to Kingsbury on the hill above the River Tame.

THE CASTLE AT KENILWORTH

WALK 8

3½ miles (5.5 km)

It was in the Wars of the Barons that Kenilworth was the centre of attraction in England's history. The great castle at Kenilworth had been given to Simon de Montfort, the barons' leader, by King Henry. The lords asked Simon to lead in battle against King Henry III — the King had antagonized the people by taking away many of the rights granted by his father, King John.

At the Battle of Lewes (1264) the royal army was routed, the King and his eldest son Edward were captured and Simon became dictator of England. The following year, Prince Edward escaped from captivity and raised an army to free his father. So we come to the Battle of Kenilworth.

Simon, the elder, who was campaigning to the west, left his son, also Simon, at Kenilworth to await fresh supplies from London. Simon the younger was no leader; his men encamped around the old green outside the castle walls and spent many hours bathing in the River Finham. There were no guards stationed and no outposts.

Edward's army, although they had been marching through the night, immediately attacked the town, surprising and routing the barons' men.

Subsequently, Prince Edward defeated Simon the elder at the Battle of Evesham and returned to lay siege to Kenilworth Castle. For six months the barons withstood the encirclement before disease and famine forced the rebels to surrender.

OPEN Kenilworth Castle is open every day except Christmas Day

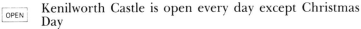 Cafés in Kenilworth and at the castle

Inns in Castle Green

Ordnance Survey 1:50,000 series, no 140

P Car Park at Castle Green

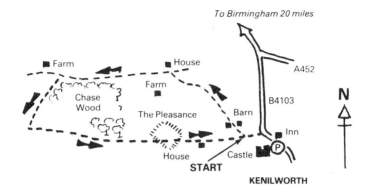

From the car park on Castle Green, take the direction of a signpost pointing along Purlieu Lane. This is a stony farm track. We go by a cottage built many centuries ago — no doubt the stone came from the castle walls!

Over a brook which once fed the great lake (which covered the acres away to our left) there is a footpath striking off to the right. Aim for the barns in the diagonal corner of the field.

Still on the same heading the track is well worn and, after twisting by a tiny copse, crosses another field to a farm lane by houses. Turn left; the way goes past a wood called Chase Wood. This is named after a renowned steeplechase of the last century. Several Roman tile kilns have been found nearby and you may find fragments today. At the end of the wood, turn left along a signposted footpath (woods now on left).

There is the spire of the village church on a far ridge — this is at Honiley and its design is said to have been influenced by Sir Christopher Wren (the architect of St Pauls, you will remember), who lived at Wroxall Abbey, a mile or so distant.

At the bottom of the slope turn 90° left. Over stiles an area of gentle hillocks, where rabbits play, is reached. In 1414, Henry V played here — he wanted a retreat away from the castle at Kenilworth and built a massive timber framed banqueting hall and pleasure house. Henry VIII obviously did not like the tranquillity and demolished the place.

By keeping on the same bearing the great castle silhouetted against the eastern sky is neared and the outward route is soon joined.

28

WARWICK

WALK 9

2½ miles (4 km)

The celebrated town planner, Sir Patrick Abercrombie, said of Warwick in 1949: 'It represents an asset to the surrounding countryside, to the Nation and to the civilised World as a beautiful survival of an English mediaeval walled town'.

The history of such a noted town as Warwick is very sketchy. We know that Aethelflaeda built a fortification on the mound at the far end of the courtyard of the present castle. This was also probably the keep of the Norman Castle, begun by William the Conqueror in 1068. The keep has now gone but the two lofty towers remain — Guy's Tower is 93 feet high and is topped by Caesar's Tower at 106 feet. (The dungeons are below Caesar's Tower.) There is much of interest at Warwick Castle, so be prepared to spend many hours exploring.

There are many other interesting buildings on this ramble around the ancient county town. The West Gate (where the walk starts) is built on a solid rock of sandstone and is first mentioned in the records in 1129. It is topped by a chapel of the fourteenth century.

Linked to the gateway are the buildings of Lord Leycester's Hospital. Originally Guild Halls, since 1571 the place has been the hospital or almshouse for a master and twelve brethren. It was founded by Robert Dudley, Earl of Leicester for 'such poor and impotent persons as shall hereafter be maimed or hurt in the wars in the service of the Queen'. Today, there are still pensioners living in the well-restored old buildings and teas can be bought here.

The collegiate church of St Mary is as grand as many cathedrals. Much was rebuilt after a disastrous fire in 1694 but the beautiful fifteenth century Beauchamp Chapel survived the conflagration.

The East Gate is topped by a chapel — St Peter's — which is now the music room of a school. Nearby is Landor House, the birthplace of the poet Walter Savage Landor, in 1775.

At the other end of Smith Street to East Gate on our walk is St John's House. Now housing a museum, it was the site of a hospital founded in the reign of Henry II to give casual lodgings and refreshment to poor wayfarers. In the seventeenth century the Stoughton family swept the old buildings away and built the elegant mansion that we see today for themselves. It is now used as a branch of the county museum specializing in folk life and costume.

In Castle Lane is Oken's House where Thomas Oken, a great benefactor of the sixteenth century lived. The black and white cottage now houses an interesting exhibition of dolls.

OPEN *Warwick Castle* is open every day, 10.00 a.m. – 5.30 p.m. *Admission* — adults £4.99, children £3.25, family £14.50 *Oken's House* (doll museum) is open weekdays 10.00 a.m. – 6.00 p.m. and Sundays 2.30 p.m. – 5.00 p.m. *Admission* — adults 75p, children 50p. *St John's House* (folk museum and museum of the Royal Warwickshire Regiment) is open weekdays (not Monday) 10.00 a.m. — 5.30 p.m. and summer Sundays 2.30 p.m. – 5.00 p.m. *Admission* — free; *Lord Leycester's Hospital* is open weekdays only, 10.00 a.m. – 5.30 p.m. *Admission* — adults £1.50, children 50p

Many cafés in the town. Refreshments available at the castle, St Nicholas Park and Lord Leycester's Hospital

Many old inns in the town

Ordnance Survey 1:50,000 series, no 151

Car parks near West Gate and in Castle Lane

I have started the walk for convenience at the West Gate. Go through the archway and note the solid sandstone rock at the base. There is a very old cast-iron letter-box through the arch. The V.R. denotes it dates from Victoria's reign — in fact it was made in 1850 and designed by Anthony Trollope.

On the left, above the terrace, is Lord Leycester's Hospital; you will probably see some of the old gentleman residents, or their wives, sitting outside.

Continue up the High Street — mainly very square Georgian architecture. Look at the patterns of the doors, no two being alike. Opposite the Court House (dating from about 1725) go along Church Street to the church of St Mary. Its tower that we are facing rises majestically to 174 feet and can be seen from far places in the vale of the River Avon. The choir is renowned and has made many popular records, especially of carols.

Retrace your steps along Church Street and cross over the High Street (once a main thoroughfare). A few steps down is the half-timbered Oken's House. The money left by Oken in trust has benefited the poor for four hundred years. Swing left; from the car park is an entrance to the past world of Warwick Castle.

After a no doubt lengthy visit to the castle, emerge through the

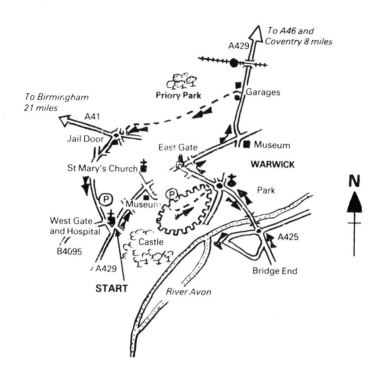

gateway on Castle Hill. Turn right for two lovely streets of old houses — absolutely charming, with no blemishes! First is Mill Street by the castle gateway; at the far end you can appreciate the height of Caesar's Tower, built on an enormous rock. The second street to see, the other side of the river, is Bridge End. Retrace your steps to Castle Hill going by the flowers and amusements of St Nicholas Park. (Boats can be hired here.)

Keep ahead to East Gate. A street here is called The Butts — this is where archery was practised. Swing to the right into Smith Street. The name is significant as many of the houses were once the places of armourers who set up their forges in medieval days when Warwick was a garrison town. By the traffic lights at the far end of Smith Street is St John's House and museum.

Directly opposite go down the Coventry Road. After 300 yds, by a garage, there is an entrance to Priory Park. The priory was pulled down by Thomas Fisher in the reign of Elizabeth I and replaced by 'a very fair house'. Only a few years ago this piece of the heritage of our land was somehow allowed to be taken down, the stones numbered and shipped for re-erection in the United States.

31

Keep by the left-hand edge of the park and walk to the rear of the new police station to Cape Road. Turn right to a junction of ways at North Gate (the gate has long gone!). Cross the road and walk along the road signposted as 'no through road for vehicles'. Be careful to look for the door from the prison on display on the left; there are two huge padlocks and bolts. The door was made in about 1700.

At the end of the road cross to the Globe Inn. Turn left down Theatre Street to the starting place.

HENLEY-IN-ARDEN AND BEAUDESERT CASTLE

WALK 10

★

2 or 6½ miles (3 or 10.5 km)

On this ramble from Henley-in-Arden we walk to one of the few commons in Warwickshire, at Yarningale. At Yarningale children can chase and hide in the bushes and play games on the grass. There are plenty of blackberries in the autumn and a hill on which to fly kites.

Henley has historical records dating back to the twelfth century. The adjoining village of Beaudesert was established in the previous century when Thurston de Montfort built a substantial castle on the steep knoll called The Mount. Henley grew to house the traders and users of the weekly fair held in the castle.

Thurston also built the little church below the castle site of Beaudesert which we can see today. The River Alne — tranquil enough now but once running through a bog — often prevented the worshippers of Henley reaching the church. In any case, the Henley villagers were in the ecclesiastical parish of Wootton Wawen (2 miles distant). They were allowed to build their own chapel in 1368 so that the difficult journeys to Wootton or Beaudesert did not have to be undertaken.

The de Montforts joined the barons against the king; Peter was killed along with his famous namesake, Simon, at the Battle of Evesham (1265). As a reprisal the castle and Henley town were burnt down by the Royalists. No castle remains can be found except the clear outlines of the hilltop fortifications. So Beaudesert was gone for ever; but Henley recovered and prospered and grew into an important trading town. Today there is still a weekly agricultural market.

There are also many interesting buildings — the Guild Hall by the church is Elizabethan; and there are old inns, many with extensive stabling beyond arched gateways. You might be interested in one timbered building — the home of the celebrated Henley Ice Cream!

Cafés in Henley-in-Arden (Tudor ices are delicious)

Inns in Henley-in-Arden and Preston Bagot

33

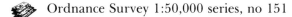 Ordnance Survey 1:50,000 series, no 151

℗ High Street Henley

From Henley go down Beaudesert Lane adjoining the church. Cross the river bridge; just beyond Beaudesert church (note the finely carved rounded Norman doorway as you pass) there is a metal gate to 'The Mount'. A puffing climb and you can become 'King of the Castle'!

Keep along the ridgetop, then climb the next hill to stiles. Now decide whether you want to curtail the ramble. For the *shortened route* climb this stile and stay on the ridgetop for a few hundred yards. The path is over stiles then bearing slightly left drop down the slope to the diagonal corner in the vale. Following waymarks walk over the next field aiming to the right of a large house. Here there are stiles to a house drive. Turn right and go 'under' an old railway bridge with no top. After about 100 yards there is a house drive on the left. Alongside is a metal kissing gate and a footpath. Walk to the far end of a pasture. Keep ahead through further meadows along an undefined path.

Still on much the same heading we are now aiming towards a factory building near the obsolete railway embankment. Over the River Alne we reach the A34 and Henley.

For the *longer walk* go over the fence stile to the right on the early hilltop. Follow the direction of electricity lines to a stile onto a lane. Turn left at Kite Green (163663), and after about ½ mile, there is a road junction where our way is to the right.

A footpath is signposted through a metal gate on the left. Walk to the diagonal corner where there is a fence-stile to climb. Keep the pool just to your right and aiming towards a house go to a large oak. Under the spreading branches is a fence-stile and you continue (hedge on right) along a path to the right of a house.

Aiming towards a church, climb stiles. We reach the little place of worship of Preston Bagot. This is the church of All Saints

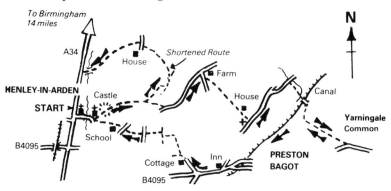

which was sited on this fair hill by the Normans — we can admire their windows and doorways still. Walk through the churchyard to a lane. Turn left (174660) and down a hill is a ford and a brook, where you can cool your feet!

Go through the nearby white metal gate on the right and keep by the stream which meanders through lush meadows. Tread quietly and you may be rewarded as I was, by the lovely blue flash of a kingfisher. Never far from the brook go through a metal gate then continue to another which leads to a bridge over the water; there is more water ahead — the Stratford Canal. Cross to the metal gate to a meadow. (Note the gap in the middle of the bridge where the towing ropes were passed to avoid unhitching the horses.)

Walk diagonally over the field to a gateway (no gate) made of railway sleepers. Over a rough bridge, turn left immediately and go up the hillside (hedge on left). This way leads to Yarningale Common.

For the return journey retrace your steps to the Stratford Canal where you turn left and walk along the towing path in a south-west direction. Please take care on the towing path not to damage the banks of this lovely waterway once owned by the National Trust.

Stay by the canal for about 1 mile; we leave it at Preston Bagot where there is the timber-framed, sixteenth-century manor house and the ancient inn. Walk along the B4095 to the crossroads at Preston Green (168653). Turn to the right to walk along a 'no through lane'. The tarmac soon peters out by a footpath sign. Keep ahead to pass in front of a cottage.

The main track swings 90° left; take care here to keep straight ahead through a field gate. In the meadow keep by the hedge to a stile in the corner. Over this and keeping on the same heading, go half-way across the next field. Turn 90° left to walk down the centre of the field to a stile, to a hedged track — an old British road.

Turn right for 50 yards. There is then another stile to climb on the opposite side of the track. Again in a field, stay by the right hand hedge. Passing a further stile we come to a field gate and lane. Almost opposite, over a fence stile the path resumes. The hedge is on your right to a stile to an adjacent pasture. A step or two under a dead tree, climb the stile.

We now overlook the vale of the Alne with Henley still guarded by the high lands of Beaudesert and the castle of the de Montforts. Drop down the bank to an estate road. Cross to a pathway which leads by a school and so to Henley. Here there are some fine inns, tearooms and many shops selling the famous Henley ices.

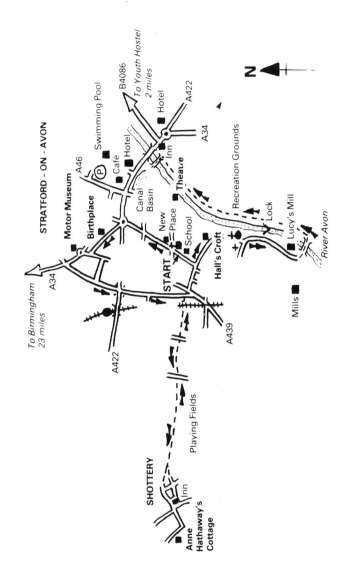

STRATFORD - ON - AVON

To Youth Hostel 2 miles

B4086

Swimming Pool

Hotel

A422

A34

Motor Museum

A46

Cafe

Hotel

Inn

Birthplace

Recreation Grounds

Canal Basin

Theatre

Lock

Lucy's Mill

New Place

School

River Avon

START

Hall's Croft

To Birmingham 23 miles

A34

Mills

A422

A439

Playing Fields

SHOTTERY

Inn

Anne Hathaway's Cottage

N

SHAKESPEARE'S STRATFORD-ON-AVON

WALK 11

5 miles (8 km)

Stratford-on-Avon is an attractive old market town and it is remarkable that so many connections with Shakespeare survived during the hundreds of years when there were few tourists to stimulate preservation of the old. Now, of course, there are so many tourists that one can only advise that you visit the place out of season, when most of the historic buildings are still open.

The birthplace of William Shakespeare is in Henley Street. It is fronted directly on to the street and the half-timbered early sixteenth century building contains many relics, and has been restored with great skill to its old appearance.

In the centre of the town is the grammar school where Shakespeare learned to love books and reading. The building dates from 1428 as the home of a religious Guild which was established in 1296 to further learning and religion. The Guild Chapel is attached to the school.

Across the road is where the great man died. The present New Place is from 1702 when rebuilt by Sir John Clopton. Shakespeare's old house of New Place was purchased by a clergyman, the Rev Gastrell, in 1753. He became weary of folk asking about 'Shakespeare's house' and the famous mulberry tree so he promptly cut the tree down and left the town. Annoyed further by having to pay rates on an empty house, he pulled the historic structure down in 1759 and so only the foundations remain today.

Harvard House (1596) is also in the centre of the town (this is not connected with Shakespeare). The mother of John Harvard who founded the great Harvard University in the USA lived here.

The church containing Shakespeare's tomb is on a lovely site beside the River Avon and is usually photographed framed by billowing willow trees. The tower is very old — perhaps 1300 — with the graceful spire added in 1763. The church holds the register which records Shakespeare's baptism on 26 April 1564.

A little upstream from the church is the Memorial Theatre. The building dates from 1932. The first Stratford Theatre was an octagon built for the great actor Garrick's Festival in 1769. The first permanent theatre was built in 1827 and the simple place was replaced towards the end of the century. A great fire destroyed

37

this theatre in 1928 — a few walls were incorporated at the back of the new building, and the adjoining library and art gallery survived the flames.

Also on this walk we go over the fields to Shottery. It is here that we see Anne Hathaway's famous cottage where the thatch curves low over the windows. It was visited by Shakespeare when he courted Anne and must have looked much the same in those days.

I have only mentioned some of Stratford's places of interest; keep your eyes open on the walk and there is history at every turn. In addition, several exhibitions, both associated with and divorced from Shakespeare, can be visited.

OPEN   *Shakespeare's houses* — most are open every day of the year; *Birthplace and Anne Hathaway's Cottage* — adults £2.00, children 80p; *New Place, Hall Croft* — adults £1.70, children 70p; *Motor Museum* is open daily. *Admission* — adults £2.00, children £1.50; (family tickets available at each place)

Cafés in Stratford

Inns in Stratford and Shottery

Ordnance Survey 1:50,000 series, no 151

Car parks are plentiful in town

From the Guild Chapel and grammar school go along Church Street (away from the chapel). On the right is New Place with its ancient well and neat gardens. We pass by the heavy black timbered Shakespeare Hotel to the High Street; keep ahead. There may be an American Stars and Stripes flag on a gabled house on the left. This is Harvard House.

At the flower-bedecked roundabout, turn left by Barclay's bank. This is Henley Street; Shakespeare's birthplace is on the right. At the end of Henley Street the Motor Museum is a step or two to the right; then retrace your steps along Windsor Street. Take the first turning on the right (Mansell Street). At the T-junction turn left and go straight over traffic lights along Grove Road.

When another main road joins, by a public garden (Evesham Place), there is a footpath signposted on the right. This way crosses a railway and a recreation ground to Shottery and Anne Hathaway's Cottage. (There is also a nice old inn here.)

Go back to Evesham Place, cross the two main roads (gardens on your left) and walk along Chestnut Walk. (There is no name board but you cannot mistake the chestnut trees on your left side!) Keep ahead (seventeenth-century Croft School on right) by the old 'core' of the town — appropriately called Old Town! We go by Hall Croft where Shakespeare's daughter lived — obviously, from the rather grand house, she was of some standing. So we come to Holy Trinity Church — a peaceful place, with the snugness of lofty trees.

At a T-junction swing left along a lane signposted 'no through road'. When the road ends keep straight on along a footpath to the river. There was always a mill here (Lucy's Mill). Now we only have some rather too-modern flats. Cross the river over the footbridge and turn left.

Staying by the bankside we come to the first lock on the Avon. This was rebuilt from the old rotting lock a few years ago by volunteer and prison labour. Beyond the lock, on the opposite bank, is the famous Stratford Memorial Theatre, which incorporates the new Swan Theatre.

Turn left over a brick bridge which was designed for the horse tramway — a line which ran from Stratford to Shipston-on-Stour. Upstream is Clopton Bridge — fourteen arches — named after its builder, Hugh Clopton, in 1490. He was to become Lord Mayor of London a year or two later.

Over the river are some beautiful gardens to end the walk. Here there is a lock to the Stratford Canal (the canal was owned by the National Trust until recently). There are steamer trips and rowing boats can be hired if you still have some energy at the end of this walk!

CLIMBING 1,000 FEET TO THE TOP OF THE LICKEY HILLS

WALK 12

12 miles (19 km)

It is said that on a clear day twelve counties of England can be seen from the top of the Lickey Hills. Actually the highest point is recorded at 987 feet above sea level but one can stand on a tower to go that little bit higher!

The walk starts at Beacon Hill — in days long ago this was one of a network of uplands used as signal stations. The fires would be lit in times of national danger such as invasion. No doubt smoke and flames went up from Beacon Hill when the Spanish Armada was nearing the coast.

The hills of Lickey are what is known as a watershed — in fact one of the main watersheds of England. The springs on one side flow eastwards to the North Sea; the waters from springs only a few hundred yards away travel south-west to the Bristol Channel.

We walk over much land that was given to the City of Birmingham by Cadburys — the chocolate family. The area is now a great 'playground' for the people who live in the city, for here there are facilities for golf, tennis and bowls, as well as fine gardens and pools to admire.

To the railway traveller in the days of steam, the Lickey incline was a notorious climb where engines had to be 'double-banked' because of the steep gradients. The horses pulling the coaches on the toll road to Bromsgrove also had difficulty; on the walk we pass by the old Rose and Crown Inn where extra horses were kept to help the coaches negotiate the hill.

There is a little nature trail incorporated into this ramble. Look out for stout posts about 3 feet high — these indicate the eight stops.

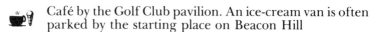 Café by the Golf Club pavilion. An ice-cream van is often parked by the starting place on Beacon Hill

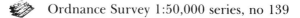 Ordnance Survey 1:50,000 series, no 139

🅿 Beacon Hill off B4096

The walk begins by the toposcope viewing tower platform (originally erected by the Cadbury family in

40

1911 but recently rebuilt). The first post is reached by walking between the toilet blocks. As you go into a plantation of Scots Pine trees (planted in 1910) you will see the trees on the exposed position are small and stunted. Some trees have a white coating of resin which has oozed from the trees. There may be clusters of twigs high in the branches indicating a magpie's nest or squirrel's drey. We can see the triangulation plinth (used by map makers) through the trees.

Post no 2 is at the bottom of the wood. The land sloping away in front of us, which for many years was pasture for sheep, is now becoming recovered by native plants such as small oaks and birches and undergrowth of brambles, heathers and bilberries. In the distance between two hills, we can just peep at the Upper Bittell reservoir built by the canal builders to 'top-up' waters lost in the locks. The hills are of a 'pre-Cambrian' rock — one of the oldest in the world.

Swing right to take the lower of two paths. Cross a patch of grass and another track to post no 3. We are now on a path between two plantations (mainly Scots pine on right). Apparently 20 years ago some trees were cut down when suffering from an attack by the pine beetle. With the increased light the grass, brambles and willowherbs have found a ready home in the open patches.

Bear left away from the main path to post no 4. There are larches ahead — the larch is one of the few conifers that lose their needles in winter. They look especially attractive in spring when they have their new 'coats' of a delicate green hue. Near the post there is an area of natural growth — we can see the gorse which usually has some yellow flowers at any time of the year.

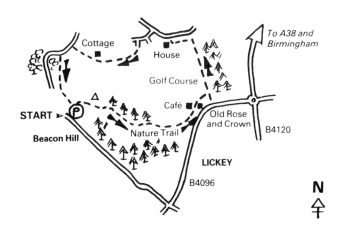

Turn left and, after about 150 yards, you come to post no 5. Look down the 'ride' or gap between plantations to the golf course. This was once farmland. The trees in the wood on the left are Scots pines — the only cone-bearing tree native to the British Isles. On the right are mainly Norwegian spruce (Christmas trees). Their cones are usually borne at the top and make good decorative features if collected and sprayed with paint.

Turn right and walk downhill. You go by a bank — the remnants of a field hedge which was once 'cut and laid'. You will notice that the trees in the shelter of the valley become taller and the undergrowth is vigorous where light comes through gaps in the trees.

We go over a tiny stream — the infant River Arrow — and turn left; post no 6 is here. You will see a large sycamore with two trunks. Notice that many tree trunks, because of the constantly damp and cool atmosphere, have a coat of pale green algae. On the left pass hazel bushes — they have beautiful catkins in spring and nuts in autumn, and elders whose fruit is gathered by home winemakers.

Further down the path is post no 7. The brook here has been widened to form the watercress pool. Tall yellow wild iris and spiraeas also grow here. Cross the water so pools are on your right side. There are masses of daffodils here in springtime. Post no 8 is at the bridge at the head of the big pool. The larger tree by the bridge is a balsam poplar from Canada and British trees that love water, the alder and willow, are nearby. There are fish in the pool and they may rise to snatch pieces of bread. Also on the pool are water-fowl — moorhens, mallard ducks and geese.

The walk continues past the café and golf shop. Keep the golf course on your left as you go through the car park. Climb to a bold track and turn left so golfers still play on your left. About 50 yards before a road, go through a hedge gap on the left. Keep at the side of the golf course until confronted by a house. Here gain the road on your right and turn left.

Take the first road left (Valley Farm Road). Look for Links Drive and, at the end of the cul-de-sac, climb a stile to the golf course again. Turn right and walk by a cottage to a lane. Here our way is left for 200 yards. There is now a clear track to climb, slowly no doubt, to the top of Beacon Hill. Perhaps that ice-cream van will be there!

THE HIDING PLACES OF HARVINGTON HALL

WALK NO 13

5½ miles (9 km)

There is nothing like a rambling and gaunt house with creaking floors and doors and surrounded by a moat to set the imagination going. But when you add the many secret hiding-places, and such ingenious ones, the imagination runs riot! There may not be ghosts at Harvington Hall but there are plenty of tales of intrigue and interest in this jumble of a house.

Harvington Hall as we know it dates from the time of the Tudors but has had much added to it since those days. Also the original timber-framed house was incorporated into the main structure, the work of Humphrey Packington, in about 1580. Humphrey's ancestor, Sir John Packington, was a judge much favoured by King Henry VIII. So much favoured, apparently, that he could remain with his head covered in the monarch's presence!

With the Reformation, Humphrey does not appear to have given up the Catholic faith as required by law. Only eight years after building the house, he had constructed (probably under the guise of repair and alteration work) the magnificent hiding places for the Roman Catholic priests.

The enlarged hall was a most irregular shape and lent itself to the ingenuity of the builders. My special favourite is the space reached by lifting false stairs — from here the hider could spy on visitors in the hall lobby.

The thought of more undiscovered hiding places is always in the minds of children as they look around the rooms on different levels. Unlikely, but who knows in this fascinating place?

The walk starts at Chaddesley Corbett where the main street has an enviable reputation of being one of the most attractive in the county, with its many old black-and-white buildings so typical of Worcestershire. The church, with its prominent spire and Norman work, has an unusual dedication — to St Cassian. It is said to be the only one in the country so called. Cassian was a schoolmaster in the reign of Diocletian and was stabbed to death by the pens of his pagan pupils.

| OPEN | *Harvington Hall* is open (except December and January) Tuesdays to Sundays 2.00 — 6.00 p.m. |

☕ Tearoom at Harvington Hall

🍺 Inns in Chaddesley Corbett and Harvington

📖 Ordnance Survey 1:50,000 series, no 139

🅿 Road is wide and quiet by church

▬ From the church go along the A448 towards Kidderminster. Walk by a black-and-white farmhouse which has been here since the sixteenth century. After ¼ mile, cross over brooks and turn right by the village hall. Walk along a farm drive between greenhouses. In a field which is sometimes cultivated with sugar beet, keep ahead and aim just to the left of a corrugated iron barn. Here, there is a stile and a vehicle track.

Immediately after a five-bar gate, turn off the vehicle track through a gap in the hedge on your left and proceed up the incline by an electricity post. At a grassy farm track, with the buildings of New House Farm on your right, cross almost straight over to walk with a hedge on your right side.

Climb a fence-stile next to a metal gate (boundary on right side). Where the hedge bends slightly to the left go over the fence stile (may be a little broken). Regain the former direction alongside the old hedge which is now on your left. When the hedge ends keep on the same heading — no hedge now but usually the line is denoted by being the boundary of two different crops.

Pick up the line of an obsolete hedge on your right-hand side. Turn 90° left in the corner along a tractor way so the hedge is still on your left.

Walk along the farm vehicle track (hedge on left side) and so to Harvington Hall. There is a large scale map of the footpaths of the area — about 6 inches to the mile — by the hall entrance so you can check your route!

Resuming the ramble, proceed along the lane by the little Catholic church. The lane divides here and to the left is the short way back to Chaddesley Corbett. For the longer route (on which there is a path which can be a little tricky) take the right fork.

At the main road turn right. After about ¼ mile take the turning to the left by school playing fields. There is a crossroads where our way is left. On top of a ridge, after ¼ mile, and opposite a metal gate and scrubland, there is an unsignposted pathway on the left. Climb to the top of the bank and go through the gap in the hedge. Walk away from the road past an isolated yew tree. Continue down the slope to go through a large metal gate under an oak tree.

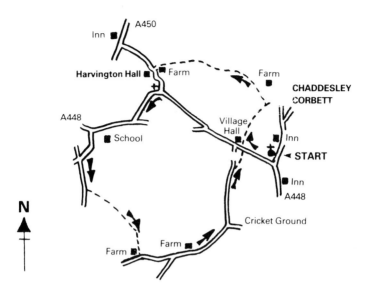

Bear right to another gate to a large pasture. Aim to the left of a large brick house. Join a farm track here for the few yards to the road. Turn left then left again at junctions. At the ground of CCCC, Chaddesley Corbett Cricket Club, you may be fortunate to be able to see some exciting village cricket.

Nearing the main road, look for a well-used footpath by a black gate on the right. A final right turn on the A448 and you will see the 'marker' of the lofty church spire.

BUILDINGS FROM THE PAST—AVONCROFT

WALK 14

4 miles (6.5 km)

For 1,000 years windmills and watermills were man's largest and most complex working machines — the power from running water was used by the Greeks in the first century BC. The use of the wind to do work was a more recent discovery — perhaps by Arabs in the seventh century — and was brought to these shores by returning Crusaders, in the twelfth century.

With the advent of steam power in the eighteenth century their usefulness declined. Who knows, perhaps with the shortage of fossil fuels in the world, we may see a rebirth of windmills.

As mills fell into disuse they were pulled down, with only the many Windmill Hill names on the map to show their sites, turned into quaint houses or left to the destructive power of the elements. One such derelict mill was saved from complete ruin in 1969 and re-erected at the Avoncroft Museum of Buildings. Today it is the centrepiece of a fascinating collection and the start of this walk.

The mill at Avoncroft is known as the Danzey Green Windmill, after the hamlet in Warwickshire where it stood. It is a post mill, where the whole working top rotates on a post to face the prevailing wind. The mill is thought to date from about 1800 and was used to grind corn. It is again in working order and if you are lucky enough to call on the right day you can see the flour being manufactured in the old fashioned way.

There are many other buildings of interest to see at Avoncroft — for example, old craftsmen's shops such as a nailer's and chain maker's workshops and a black-and-white inn.

Also on this walk we go to Stoke Prior — the church in the wood has a window monument to philanthropist industrialist, John Corbett, who ordered in 1860 that no longer would women and young girls work in the local salt pits. The nearby brook is the 'Salwarpe' — a river of salt.

Towards the end, near Bromsgrove, the railway is crossed. In the days of steam the line from here was famous as the Lickey Incline — it was one of the most difficult railway hills in England and trains were double-banked from this point to negotiate the steep 1 in 40 slope.

46

Avoncroft Museum of Building is open from March to November, daily 11.00 a.m. — 6.00 p.m. *Admission* — adults £2.30, children £1.15

Café in Avoncroft

Inns in Stoke Prior

Ordnance Survey 1:50,000 series, nos 139 and 150

P Car park in Avoncroft

From the car park turn left to the A4024 on Buntsford Hill, then left along the main road. By the drive of Avoncroft College there is a footpath signposted through a kissing gate on the left. Cut over a meadow and sports field to the B4091, where you turn left. Just past the Ewe and Lamb Inn, there is a bridleway signposted down a vehicle track on the left. You will now have a good view of the Avoncroft Windmill silhouetted against a pastoral skyline.

The bridleway drops down to the River Salwarpe and continues to a lane. A step or two to the right a footpath is signposted to the church and the B4091 again. Proceed to the left and stay on this road, passing road junctions and going under the railway, to the canal bridge at Stoke Wharf. In the Canal Age this was a busy 'port' for the loading and unloading of cargoes.

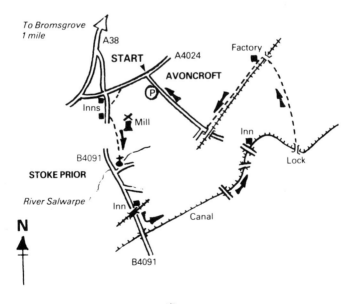

On the towing path walk left, away from the road, in a north-easterly direction. Past locks we go by a waterside inn. (The sign reminds us of the long reign of Queen Victoria.) A long flight of locks begins — this is the famous Tardebigge flight (see Tardebigge, Walk 15).

Just before the canal twists around the corner there is a railing bridge over the lock where you cross the waterway. Just to the right is a hedge going up an incline and away from the canal; this is our way. Proceed, keeping the hedge on your right-hand side. At the summit of the hill swing slightly left to descend, keeping a soil dumping ground in an old quarry on the right. Drop down to a bold stile to a field (sometimes under the plough). Walk alongside a right-hand hedge. This direction is towards a factory building and takes us to a bridge over the railway.

Immediately over, turn left to keep by the railway along a tarmac pathway (car park on right) which leads to a lane. Turn right and climb the hill to Avoncroft and the buildings from the past.

TARDEBIGGE — ONE OF THE WONDERS OF BRITAIN

WALK 15

★

5 miles (8 km)

In a book published on the wonders of Britain a few years ago, the name of Tardebigge appeared. Tardebigge is a hamlet a mile or so from Bromsgrove and consists solely of a church, a large rectory and a school — each attractive in their own ways and full of interest but hardly 'wonders'. No, it is the canal in the vale that has brought fame to Tardebigge over the centuries.

In the canal days, Tardebigge meant hard work for the bargees; the area is hilly and the industrial conurbation of the Midlands is on the top of a plateau about 400 feet above sea level. It was at Tardebigge that a huge flight of locks was constructed by an army of navvies to haul the craft up the incline before the tunnel through the hillside.

This stretch of the Worcestershire and Birmingham Canal was opened in 1815 after 25 years of petulant construction. Shortage of water was the continued problem. Although huge reservoirs were created from damming valleys the water loss from the large number of locks was great.

On the Tardebigge stretch vessels climb 220 feet in 2½ miles and the flight is rightly considered the finest in the land. The Tardebigge top lock is the deepest narrow lock in England with a 14 feet fall. Today, the holiday craft ply this stretch but the continual opening and closing of heavy lock gates is anything but a holiday!

The church of Tardebigge is on top of a green hill and the slender spire rises to 135 feet and is a gracious landmark for miles around. The building was built in 1777 and replaced a church which had collapsed a year or so before. The Saxons chose the site and the rather strange name could well have come from the Saxon 'Tyrde Biegan' — Tower on a Hill.

The school is nearby; we read that one of the pupils in the seventeenth century was John Heydon. Later, besides being a lawyer, he dabbled in astrology. He foretold that Cromwell would die by the rope. Cromwell ordered Heydon's book be destroyed and that Heydon be confined to Lambeth House.

☕ Cafés in Bromsgrove (start of walk is actually at Aston Fields 1 mile from town centre)

🍺 Inn in Aston Fields

📚 Ordnance Survey 1:50,000 series, no 139

🅟 Park in streets off the main road

By Bromsgrove Station on the B4184, go along the nearby St Godwalds Road. At a T-junction of lanes by a farm turn left (Dusthouse Lane), then almost immediately right. The lane is signposted to Stoke Pound. Just beyond a railed bridge over a brook, go through double gates on the left.

Keep by the left-hand hedge (but do not go through the metal gate). In the corner, by a wire fence, climb a stile. *Warning:* the stile may be overgrown and you may have to use the gate a yard or so to the right of the corner.

Beyond the stile stay by the left-hand boundary at the edge of an arable field. The way bears slightly right as it goes up the hillside. Near the top of the ridge is a crossing hedge. Go through the gate on the left, then regain the old heading but with a hedge now on your right side.

You now reach the canal by locks of the Tardebigge flight. Turn left along the towing path. As the tunnel entrance is approached, there is a lock-keeper's cottage. Alongside the garden is a stile and a sharp climb up the hill-pasture to St Bartholomew's church, Tardebigge.

Retrace your steps to the lock-keeper's cottage and the nearby bridge over the waterway. Leave the towing path by climbing

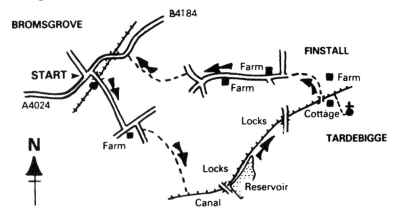

stiles and walking over the bridge and into a pasture. Bear right to go down the slope, keeping well to the left of a pool, to a stile in the far right-hand corner. Go down the bank. Bear left to follow a tiny rivulet downstream and climb a new stile.

In the far left-hand corner of the field where horses gallop, is a footpath sign. Go over the bridge across a ditch. Swing left to go by a bank topped by bushes. A farm vehicle track is met; this leads to a lane. Turn left, go by Dusthouse Farm and keep ahead at the junction along Dusthouse Lane. This is a narrow lane now with another ancient building, Stonehouse Farm, which is black and white with a Tudor overhang. At a crossroad turn right. There is soon a footpath indicated on the left over a stile. This way is fenced each side and takes us to the parkland of Finstall Park. This track stays by the right-hand boundary and bears gradually around to the right and over a stile. Continue on to the main road; the walk is just about completed with the station at Aston Fields, to the left.

ADVENTURE AT RAGLEY HALL

WALK 16

★

4 miles (6.5 km)

Ragley Hall is the home of the Marquess and Marchioness of Hertford. The building is a magnificent mansion of Palladian style, so called after the ideas of an Italian architect, Andrea Palladio (1518–80).

The hall dates from the seventeenth century and contains a wonderful collection of old paintings and furniture together with a recent work of art — a huge mural alongside the main staircase. It is all very stately, but it is outside that you can have fun. There is a magnificent adventure playground where high ropeways can be walked, elaborate wooden constructions climbed and trampolines tramped on. I almost forgot the recent addition — a maze where baby brothers or fathers may get lost! If you are still bounding with energy, the country nature trail is full of interest.

Alcester, where the walk starts, was a Roman town where Roman finds (coins, brooches and pottery) have been unearthed. The way of the legionnaires from the station at Wall in Staffordshire to Stow on the Wold, Ryknild Street, passes through the town.

There are many old and quaint buildings in the town which was once a centre for needle-making, using the power of the two modest rivers — the Arrow and the Alne. Butter Street is charming, and nearby is the seventeenth century town hall — no doubt it was once open on the ground floor for noisy market traders selling their wares.

OPEN *Ragley Hall* is open from April to September, daily, except Mondays and Fridays, but open Bank Holiday Mondays. *Admission* — park (including adventure wood and country trail) — adults £2.50, children £1.50, (house and maze extra)

Cafés at Ragley Hall and in Alcester town

Inns in Alcester

Ordnance Survey 1:50,000 series, no 150

Car parking in High Street, Alcester

The way out of Alcester is along Bleachfield Street, across the busy A422 from the High Street. Bleachfield Street is bordered by cottages built 200 years ago.

At the end of a new housing estate on the right, walk along the vehicle drive between a wood fence and a wire fence to a stile alongside a gate. In the field walk diagonally to the left to a stile and railed footbridge. Still on the same heading, we reach the River Arrow bending a tranquil way through the meadows. Away to the left is Primrose Hill — capped by huge rocket-like silos for the storage of animal food.

Over Spittle Brook keep straight ahead (river still on left) and through a hedge gap, cross an embankment. You may hear the sound of ghost trains in the breeze — steam trains on the way to Evesham used to pass this way. (A new road is under construction here — the path may be diverted.)

Over the new road and again in a field, stay on the same direction — you will see a stile and bridge over a stream. Cut over the meadow, crossing a tarmac church path and pass just to the left of an ancient animal shelter. (The church is the Norman Arrow church and contains memorials to the Seymours — the family name of the Marquess of Hertford.)

Bearing slightly left, go over a vehicle drive to a stile, plank bridge and metal kissing gate. To the right now are the elegant gates to Ragley Hall — the great house can just be seen peeping over the ridge. Away to the left, on a hilltop is Oversley Castle — a country mansion. The old castle, a wooden affair erected by Ralph de Boteler in the twelfth century, was on a knoll behind Arrow Mill.

53

Arrow Mill was once a large corn mill and is now a fashionable restaurant where the wheel turns to amuse the diners. There is a metal gate to the mill drive and we come to the A435 main road to the right. Through the main gates of Ragley, the drive meanders through the parkland of old oak trees to the hall where there is so much to enjoy.

Retrace steps to the A435 and turn left to Arrow Village. By the cottages and old toll house take the A422 on the left. Stay on this road for ¼ mile. There is then a signposted footpath on the right, opposite woods and by a stream. Keep by the hedge and pass through a metal gate by a fast stream. Turn right and over the brook to follow the waters downstream.

After about 150 yards do not go through the wooden gate but turn left to walk up the incline (hedge on right). At the end of a field there are cattle pens and a gateway. Through the gateway cross the field in a diagonal direction across a new road to a footbridge over Spittle Brook. A few steps further is a stile to climb. Still on the same heading is another stile by houses. Children in these houses can almost say 'a railway ran through the middle of our house!'

When you reach Roman Way turn left then right (Augustus Drive). By house no 11 go along the tarmac pathway back to the town the Romans built.

EVESHAM FERRY

WALK 17

★

2 miles (3 km)

Evesham is one of those towns in the land that seems to have almost a surfeit of history. It abounds in interest from the time when Eoves, the swineherd, found the favoured site and gave the place its name — Eoveshome, hence Evesham.

The town stands on a narrow sweep of the River Avon; it is said Eoves saw a vision of Our Lady and with great speed went to convey the news to his bishop, Egwin. The holy man was impressed and began his great abbey by the river. The building took six years and the bishop died there in 717. The town was outside the walls of the monastery.

By the starting place of the walk was the great abbey; there are now three lofty buildings. The Bell Tower is the finest surviving section of the abbey. It was the last part built by Abbot Lichfield and completed in 1539 — the same year that Henry VIII decreed the dissolution of the abbey. The tower was in a dangerous state until restored in 1951 and there is a lovely carillon which sounds sweetly over the town.

Nearby, are two churches only a few yards apart. Why two? Well, it is said that the older, All Saints, was for the people of Evesham, while the other, St Lawrence, was for the pilgrims who visited the abbey. In the gardens near the Bell Tower is a plinth marking the place of the high altar of the abbey — the last resting place of Simon de Montfort.

Fifty years before, in 1215, the great barons forced King John to sign the Magna Carta. The government of England had become a mockery and the barons thought that the declaration would restore a semblance of democracy. This was not to be, however, as John's successor, Henry III, eroded the terms of the Magna Carta.

Simon de Montfort, once Henry's chief advisor, joined the barons to fight the dictatorial monarch. In 1260 de Montfort was elected to lead the rebels in their fight to restore the rights of the people. We now read the end of the story on the plinth 'Here were buried the remains of Simon de Montfort, Earl of Leicester, pioneer of representative government, who was killed in the Battle of Evesham on August 4th1265.' The stone was brought from his birthplace — the castle of Montfort L'Amoury in France and was erected to commemorate the 700th anniversary of his death.

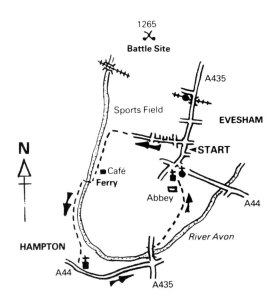

The abbey was dissolved by Henry VIII in 1539 and, apart from the Bell Tower, little remains of the great building. There is a fragment of wall and an archway near the tower and, by the main road, is the Almonry Museum. It was here that the alms of the abbey were given; today it has a fascinating collection of local antiquities. Outside are the stocks which were once in the town gaol.

Before starting the ramble from the museum, glance across at the working men's club over the road. The building is modern except for the porch. This looks Tudor and indeed is — through this archway passed the pupils at the Grammar school endowed by the great Abbot Lichfield.

OPEN   *Almonry Museum* is open daily *Admission* — 50p, (children free); *Hampton Ferry* operates daily — *Fares:* adults 10p, children 5p

Cafés in Evesham town and by Hampton Ferry

Inns in Evesham and Hampton

Ordnance Survey 1:50,000 series, no 150

Car parks in Evesham

From the Almonry Museum walk northwards along the High Street. We go by the Market Place but a little detour can be made to the Norman gateway which connected the town to the churchyards. No 51 High Street is Dresden House — the rains of hundreds of years have run through the elegant lead pipes dated 1622.

Opposite the early Georgian Star Gazer Inn, turn left down Avon Street. We go by the markets where produce from the Vale — the market garden of the Midlands — is sold. Keep ahead, crossing other streets and staying by a sports field. Glance to the distant hill to the right — it was on this upland that the great battle took place in 1265.

At the river turn left to follow the placid waters upstream. There are fine fishing places here with good cover. We come to the Hampton Ferry and call across for the ferryman — travellers have used this place for many hundreds of years. The ferryman pulls the craft by hauling on a fixed rope.

Safely over the water, turn left, keeping on the bankside. Climb a stile to a rough pasture where friendly horses will welcome some attention! At the far end of the field climb the stile and turn right along a vehicle track to the A44. This is a busy road so take care! We go by Hampton church, the work of the Normans, with an old sundial on the tower and some ugly gargoyles leering at us. Cross the River Isbourne — a small lazy-looking brook now, but it once powered many mills before joining the Avon.

At the traffic lights turn left to cross the modern (1928) bridge. Immediately over the water go through a metal gate and walk down the steps. Go under the road where there is now a pleasant avenue of lime trees.

Almost at the far end of the avenue swing over to the left to a track by tennis courts. We are now heading towards the church spires and the abbey site and the end of the ramble.

BREDON HILL

WALK 18

★

5 miles (8 km)

In the Iron Age (about 700 BC) the occupiers of our land from the continent set up a chain of fortresses on strategic points to contain the retaliatory raids of the Welsh. One of the largest and strongest sites was perched on the 1,000 feet summit of Bredon Hill.

Bredon Hill is known to geologists as an outlier of the Cotswolds. The outline of the hill from a distance is like a huge whale emerging from the flat sea of the vale. The rock (limestone) is the same as the Cotswolds so we find a similar landscape; the old cottages are alike with the mellow yellow of the lichen-covered stone; walls that contained the sheep are cleverly constructed of layered boulders.

Villages are grouped around the base of the upland like jewels around the edge of a crown. One such charming place is Elmley Castle. The main street is fringed by a clear stream and at the end is an inn, the Queen Elizabeth (which commemorates the visit of Elizabeth I), and the church.

The castle overlooked this end of the village; built by Robert le Despenser in the eleventh century it was once the seat of the Beauchamps. It was finally in ruins by the early sixteenth century; today only the earthworks and a few chunks of stone remain.

Until a few years ago there was a great house behind the church; the seat of the Savage family. It had survived from 1600 and was said to have been a most attractive gabled residence. At the other end of the village is the weather-worn fifteenth century village cross where prayers for a safe journey over treacherous roads were offered. And most importantly, nearby is the Plough Inn which specializes in strong local cider, served, as it should be, in ceramic pots — not glasses!

If you are uncertain whether to take raincoats on this walk remember the local rhyme:

When Bredon Hill puts on his hat
Ye men of the vale, beware of that!

🏨 Inns in Elmley Castle

🗺 Ordnance Survey 1:50,000 series, no 150

🅿 In wide main street by the Queen Elizabeth Inn

58

Take the lane signposted as a no-through-road, by the Queen Elizabeth Inn. The road twists to the left by a farm; the houses are soon left behind and the land gradually goes uphill by tiny thatch-roofed cottages.

At the end of the lane continue ahead along a banked limestone track. Go through a metal field gate and continue along the farm vehicle track for about 50 yards, then cut across the undulating pastureland to a metal gate in the top left-hand corner. There are now some fine views far, far across the Evesham Vale.

Through the gate keep on the uphill trek by the broken wall on your left-hand side. The track is soon clear over a winding way through hawthorn bushes. There are huge thistles growing in this rough land of which a Scotsman would be proud! You may, like me, enjoy the sight of a deer here if you walk quietly.

At a junction of tracks by a wood keep ahead for about 30 yards (woods on left) then swing left; still climbing, go up hummocky ground where rabbits play (woods still on left). This is the steep scarp slope of Bredon Hill and geologists tell us that this has been subjected to landslips over the years, hence the uneven nature of the terrain. At a five bar gate on your left do not go through but turn 90° right to walk alongside a wire fence (on your left side now).

The River Avon is now below us with Pershore and its very prominent green-topped abbey church tower; the tiny villages look as though they had been transported from toytown. Keep by the wire to a ridge-top copse of pines. It is bounded by a 'Cotswold' wall — note the arrangement of the stones and that the wall is strong without the use of a binding mortar.

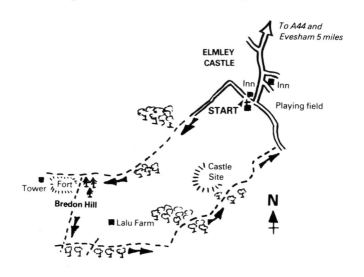

Still on the same heading (wall on left) go over a stile by a gateway at the far side of the pinewood. The earthworks of the great fort lie ahead. The occupation came to an abrupt end in the first century AD — the bodies of over fifty defenders, brutally hacked, were found in a gulley. The square tower nearby is called Parson's Folly — it was said to have been the whim of Mr Parson of Kemberton Court merely to take the hill over the 1,000 feet mark! Much folklore is associated with the hill. Just below the tower are the King and Queen Rocks and the Banbury Stone with the connotation of fertility superstitions in days long past.

Return to the copse of pine trees. Do not re-climb the stile but turn 90° right, leaving the scarp edge of the Hill. The copse is now on your left side. The Cotswolds dominate the far skyline like the great wall of China. Keep alongside the boundaries of fields, going over a farm vehicle way to the corner of an elongated wood of tall beech trees.

Turn left along a wide track (beeches now on right). Cross a tarmac way — the drive to the isolated Lalu Farm. Remain on the hard track until it swings sharp left towards a Post Office telecommunications tower. We leave the track to keep ahead alongside a plantation of Scots pines. Our track is now wide and grassy and we pick up the line of tall pines. They go to the left and so do we, towards a wood.

Walk through a field gate and continue through another to the edge of the trees. There is a crossing track beside the wood. Cross this track to take a path — slightly concealed — bearing right to go into the trees. Within a yard or so walk through a gateway (no gate) onto a nice path now — cool in summer and sheltered in winter. Immediately out of the trees take care as the way is a little obscure.

Cross a main banked track to a path directly opposite, which immediately bears right; a fine place for blackberries. There is now a clear and well-used descending track with a view through the trees on your left side. Descend through bushes to a little hunting gate to the rough edge of a field. As we descend we can see the knoll on the left on which was perched the Beauchamp's castle. The path is 'lost' for a while but keep descending down the 'V' of the valley. Follow the waymarks of the Wychavon Way. Join a tractor way but leave it after a wood. Keep to a narrow path. Do not go through a metal gate but swing left to proceed by a deep, hidden pool. The path leads to a hunting gate by a brook. Keep ahead to an often ploughed field. Stay by the right-hand boundary to a lane. To the left is Elmley Castle.

THE OLD OLYMPIC GAMES AT DOVER HILL

WALK 19

4 miles (6.5 km)

In 1610 Robert Dover, an Army Captain, organized competitive games and sports in a hilltop meadow near Chipping Campden. They became an annual event and attracted huge support from towns, cities and villages for miles around.

The activities continued for over 200 years until they officially closed in 1841. The reason, perhaps foreshadowing hooligan football supporters today, was recorded as being brutality and rowdyism. The games have been revived in recent times. The land is now owned by the National Trust and you can chase and play games where our forefathers enjoyed sports for many centuries.

The walk starts at the large village of Chipping Campden ('Chipping' is Old English for 'market place'). The wealth of the place was founded on the wool trade

The merchants left their mark in the magnificent buildings of Chipping Campden. The fifteenth-century church has the grandeur of a cathedral. Nearby the ruined manor house — Campden House — and the open market hall in the main street, are relics of the days of the first Lord Campden, Sir Baptist Hicks. At the time of the Civil War the great mansion was deliberately set on fire so that it would not fall to Cromwell's forces.

Among the notable houses in the main street is the wool merchant's house — Grevel House. There are countless other houses of honey-hued stone and a fascinating little museum. The Woolstaplers Hall Museum has an interesting array of bricabrac including a cinema of the 1920's and a nineteenth-century balloon.

 Woolstaplers Hall Museum is open daily April to September, 11.00 a.m. – 6.00 p.m. *Admission* — adults £1.00, children 50p

 Cafés in Chipping Campden

 Inns in Chipping Campden

 Ordnance Survey 1:50,000 series no 151

P   Limited car parking in main street

From the Old Wool Market Hall, walk along the main street away from the church. By the Catholic church turn right along the little lane. At a junction swing left along Hoo Lane. You will see a Cotswold Way signpost here. (The 'Way' is a long distance footpath which goes along the scarp edge of the Cotswold plateau from Chipping Campden to Bath.)

Walk past cottages of thatch and a garden with good examples of topiary ('birds' shaped from yew bushes). Also you will see on the houses with tiled roofs that the tiles are of natural stone with the traditional Cotswold grading — large tiles at the bottom of the roof and tiny ones at the ridge. A gradual climb, now on a rough bridlepath, leads to a road at the summit where there are lovely views over Campden.

Turn left along the road. After a few hundred yards there is a signposted footpath to the right. Keep at the edge of the field (sometimes cultivated) to a stile in the far right-hand corner. (To the left is the meadow of Dover's Hill and the triangulation point.) We turn right over the stile. The path is well-used and clear and soon goes through a wooden gate. We overlook a chequered countryside of many colours.

Keep along the undulating track to a road (the B4035). Turn right to a junction with the B4081. Here proceed to the left then right down a lane signposted to Hidcote Boyce. Keep along the

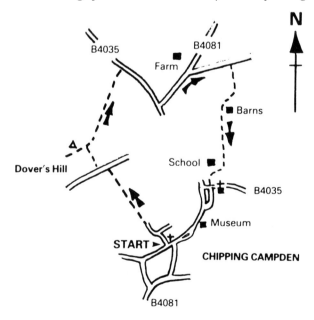

lane for about ¼ mile. Almost in a dip there are two adjacent field gates on the right (one of the gates is very wide).

Climb the stile beside the wide gate under an oak tree. Once in a field walk at the edge (hedge on your left side). Go over a plank bridge in a gap in the corner hedge. In the next field turn right and continue around the periphery to pass by a black Dutch barn. (The path is waymarked — yellow arrow.)

Keep ahead on the same heading; the path is indicated to keep just to the left of a corrugated iron grain barn. The track leads to a school playing field; keep this on your right. There is a notice at the end of the field to take us to a lane. The return to Chipping Campden is by the church and the row of almshouses of the seventeenth century.

BROADWAY TOWER COUNTRY PARK

WALK 20

5 miles (8 km)

If you like natural history, or if your taste is to climb high hills or to the top of high buildings, this is your walk. All these features are covered in the Broadway Tower Country Park perched on the steep scarp edge of the Cotswold ridge.

The charges relating to the park cover all the admission to the tower, natural history centre, the two nature trails and the excellent facilities of the park. There are several public rights of way going through the park area (including the long distance footpath, The Cotswold Way). No payment, of course, is necessary solely to use these clearly defined tracks.

The landmark of Broadway Tower is 55 feet high and was built in the eighteenth century by the sixth Earl of Coventry. It is a 'prospect tower' — structures such as these are relics of the landscaping movement of the time.

It is said the Earl used the tower to send messages to his wife at home at Croome Court, many miles away, near Upton-on-Severn. Could he really have signalled 'keep my dinner warm; I'll be late home'? Today, there is an interesting display of local history items housed in the tower, besides an observation room.

It is estimated that one of the two nature trails takes one hour to complete, the other about half an hour. They are mainly through woodlands and details can be obtained from the Rookery Barn café.

 The Broadway Tower Country Park is open every day from 31 March to 1 October, 11.00 a.m. to 6.00 p.m.

 Cafés in Broadway and in the Rookery Barn, Broadway Park

 Inns in Broadway and Fish Hill

 Ordnance Survey 1:50,000 series, no 150

 Car park off the Stratford Road, Broadway

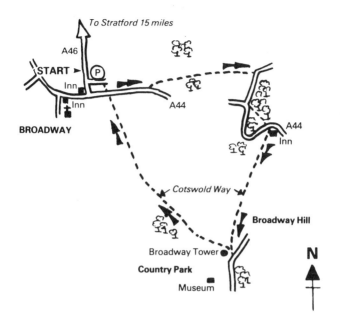

The walk starts at the show village of Broadway. It has been said to be the prettiest village in England; this is debatable, of course, but no-one can deny it is immensely picturesque, with cottages, shops and old inns of mellow stone set beyond trim grass verges. Its only detracting features are the great crowds, who have heard it is the prettiest of villages and have come to linger awhile, and the main road. Vehicles charge down Fish Hill and race through the very heart of the place at a hideous pace as though eager to get beyond Broadway as soon as possible!

From the car park take the path signposted to the High Street (by the public toilets). On a road turn left and stay on this heading to the end of the cul-de-sac road. By houses (called 'Salubrious') take the path to the right indicated by a yellow arrow to the A44 main road. Turn left and, by the speed de-restriction sign, go through a metal gate or stile on the left. Continue at the edge of a field by the left-hand boundary.

The ground is rough. Walk to the far-left corner, where there is a log stile, then immediately go through a hunting gate. Keep by the right-hand boundary to go alongside a wood of ancient trees on your right side. Beyond a metal hunting gate keep ahead (rough hedge on left). When the rough hedge ends by fallen trees (elms felled after being contaminated by Dutch elm disease), keep on the same bearing as before — you will see the stile to aim for in the opposite boundary.

There is now a steady uphill climb over sheep pastures to a stile and lane. Turn right to the main road. A yard or so to the left, leave the road again and take the vehicle track on the left. This is an old route as explained on a notice:

> The original Fish Hill highway can be seen here and serves to remind us of the condition of roads before the advent of tarmacadam. Coaches regularly used this road travelling between London and Worcester. A company called Mr. Jolly's Wagons had a station at the bottom of the hill where extra horses could be hired for the upward journey. Forming part of a gateway, halfway up the hill, is a post on which is inscribed the words 'shut off to horses here'. This used to stand outside the Fish Inn.
>
> In 1820, the road was re-directed along its present route to south of the Inn. More recently, it was moved north of the Inn and widened and the car park area was purchased by the County Council initially for this purpose. The area to the left of the old road is now owned by a security firm who have generously entered into an Agreement with the Council to make it available for public recreation.

At the top of Fish Hill is the A44. The next path is directly opposite. To the left is the Fish Inn. This was built in 1775 as a house. The vicar of Mickleton wrote his *Ode to the Fish* when it became an inn

> . . . enter courteous guests, rest here and dine
> The Fish shall spout good ale, good punch, good wine

The path goes by the barn and along a vehicle track. Through woodlands follow the waymarked path to a gate into sheep pastures. We are now on the Cotswold Way and the track is waymarked on a post over the pastures to a hunting gate which leads to Broadway Tower and Park.

The walk resumes by the hunting gate. Do not walk through again but take the arrowed way alongside a wire fence (tower on your left side). Soon pick up a waymark sign on a white post; this shows the way to a hunting gate.

Keep ahead at the edge of fields. Keep along the clear path over many stiles — we are still on the Cotswold Way here. The path goes by a beech coppice, 'moulded' by the prevailing winds from the west and, still descending, is clearly arrowed to Broadway and the welcome 'Olde English Tea Rooms'.

WINCHCOMBE CASTLES ANCIENT AND MODERN

WALK 21

½ or 5½ miles (1 or 9 km)

It was over 500 years ago that Robert Boteler chose the site for Sudeley Castle near Winchcombe. From those times little remains — a gatehouse, a dungeon tower and the Portmare Tower, the latter named after a Frenchman who was held in the tower awaiting a ransom fee. The rest of this lovely castle set in parkland is of more recent times, much of it Tudor.

But also in Sudeley Park is a castle which was built in 1979 — this is a grand battlemented affair in the children's playground. This is an exciting place and no doubt the young gentleman of the big house had a say in the design. Here you can chase up the towers or walk the battlement; if you have a vivid imagination of Normans and knights, sieges and escapades, this is the place for you!

Sudeley Castle was the home of the Seymours in Tudor days. Katherine Parr, the sixth wife of Henry VIII, survived the monarch and married Thomas Seymour. Unfortunately, Seymour was soon to lose his head and the equally unfortunate Katherine was also soon to die. She lies buried in the church near the castle.

Further on the longer walk we come to a fine example of a Roman mosaic floor. There are no attendants in the little woodland hut preserving the floor and we can just stare at the beauty of the design and marvel that it has been preserved for almost 2,000 years.

The final point of interest on this ramble is on the lofty summit of the hills at Belas Knap. This is a long barrow, estimated to be 4,000 years old. Thanks to careful restoration we are able to get a good impression of how it looked to our Stone Age ancestors. The mound of earth was opened in 1931 and a collection of skulls and flints was found in the chamber.

Winchcombe, where the ramble starts, was once a walled city in the land of Winchcombeshire within the Kingdom of Mercia. It had a great Benedictine Abbey of which little remains today;what we can see is a magnificent church built in 1470; look at those gargoyles — have you ever seen such ugly figures! One grotesque old man in a top hat looks pained as though he has just visited the dentist!

67

OPEN *Sudeley Castle* is open from April to October, 12.00 noon – 5.30 p.m. *Admission* — adults (castle and gardens) £3.75, children (including adventure playground) under 5 — free, over 6 — £1.95 (family ticket £10.00)

☕🍴 Tearoom in Evesham Road; ices from several shops

🍺 Inns in Winchcombe

🗺 Ordnance Survey 1:50,000 series, no 163

🅿 Parking in square, Winchcombe

👉 There are two walks: the shorter just takes in Sudeley Castle; the longer has a lot of uphill work but is rewarded with fine views, the Roman mosaic and Belas Knap.

From Winchcombe go along Vineyard Street — it is signposted to Sudeley Castle. Walk over the little River Isbourne and we come to the drive.This is a twisting way to the splendours of Sudeley and the fun of the adventure playground.

Afterwards, if you wish to return speedily to Winchcombe, keep alongside the car park; there is a stile beside the gate onto a lane. Turn left back to the town.

For the longer ramble, retrace your steps back along the drive to the original lane and turn left. It is signposted no through road for vehicles. After ¼ mile there is a signposted pathway on the right.

Over a field aim just to the left of a distant red-brick farmhouse. The path is over ridges — perhaps signs of ancient strip farming — to a stile. Here there is also a footbridge over a tiny stream. Again aim just to the left of the farmhouse. There is a double stile and footbridge under an electricity pylon. Across the next field make for a point on the opposite boundary about 300 yards to the left of the red-brick farmhouse.

Follow the edge of the field to the left to climb a stile in the corner. Walk the planks (over a brook) then swing right (hedge on right). After about 300 yards climb the stile in the hedge then resume the upward way but with the hedge now on your left-hand side.

Go by dead trees and nearing the summit climb a stile by a field gate to the left of a large oak tree. Keep on the climb (same heading) with the hedge still on the left. The path is to the left of the elegant Queen Anne style house of Wadfield. The Cotswolds now open up before us, each step lowering the horizon and the vistas of stretches of lovely countryside.

Gain the farm track beyond Wadfield. Nearing the cottages leave the farm track by turning right. Skirt the field (often under the plough) with boundary on your left side to gates leading to the square coppice. Here is the building with the Roman pavement.

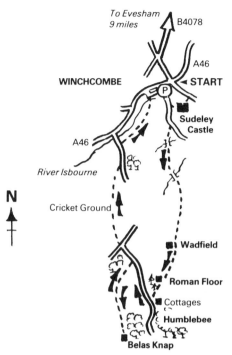

Regain the farm track and go near the cottages of Humblebee — lovely is the name and lovely is the view from here. At a lane turn right. After about ⅓ mile the path to Belas Knap Long Barrow is signposted on the left. (A pamphlet guide is on sale at Hailes Abbey — north east of Winchcombe off A46 road.)

The path to Belas Knap is well walked and clear. Return to the road and proceed to the road junction to the left. Directly opposite our lane is a stile on the banktop. Two paths are signposted. Follow the Winchcombe direction and aim for the town in the vale. Climb a stile and descend quickly over an undulating hill pasture. You should now be heading to a cricket field.

Just past an oak tree the ground levels out and there is a stile onto a farm track where you turn right. In the summer season you can stop and enjoy the cricket. Otherwise continue to the lane and turn left. After ¼ mile, as the road bends sharply to the left, climb the stile by a metal gate on the right.

In a pasture keep by the right-hand hedge. Beyond a stile by a field gate gap (no gate) continue to the far left-hand corner. Pass through a kissing gate to a football pitch — there are also swings and roundabouts. Cross the River Isbourne again and here is Winchcombe.

69

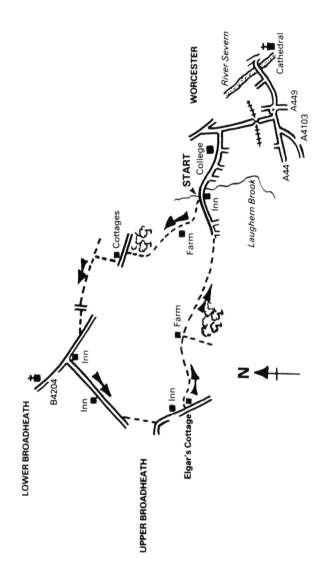

WORCESTER

River Severn

Cathedral

A449

A4103

A44

START

College

Inn

Laughern Brook

Cottages

Farm

Farm

Inn

LOWER BROADHEATH

B4204

Inn

Inn

UPPER BROADHEATH

Elgar's Cottage

N

BROADHEATH, WORCESTER

WALK 22

★

5 miles (8 km)

Worcester to the Ancient Britons was Hwicwaraceaster, the camp of the Hwiccii tribe. They chose the drained site on the eastern bank of the Severn and there was a ford near the present cathedral. The Romans knew the place as Vigornia (some records say Vertis) but it was in the late seventh century when its favoured situation was truly appreciated — a new see (diocese) was created.

By the fourteenth century there were monastic settlements of Greyfriars, Blackfriars, Franciscans and Dominicans, so by medieval times the city was the fifth largest in the realm. The wealth was founded on clothmaking; the chronicler Leland wrote 'The Welthe of the towne stands the most on draping and noe towne of England, at this present tyme, makes so many cloathes yearly'.

But, of course, Worcester is essentially the cathedral and, in spite of some generally considered unsympathetic restoration of the last century, the place is a superb example of the early-English style.

This walk is on the west side of the city, over the great stone bridge built by John Gwynn of Shrewsbury in 1771–80, for the sum of £30,000. No doubt this was a great expenditure two hundred years ago! Also, over the bridge is the riverside ground of Worcestershire County Cricket Club — surely no ground has such a magnificent back-cloth as this with the towering cathedral on the opposite bank.

The walk takes us to the village of Upper Broadheath — a rather nondescript place it is admitted, except for the fact that it was here that Sir Edward Elgar, one of the most revered composers in the land, was born. Ten years or so ago the tiny cottage of brick was opened to the public as a fascinating museum. Here, there are mementos of the composer, his manuscripts and letters, the honours that were bestowed on him by a seemingly reluctant nation. The graceful uplands of the Malvern Hills can be seen from his cottage garden. He was laid to rest at a chapel at Little Malvern in the shadow of the hills.

 Elgar Museum, Upper Broadheath, is open every day (except Wednesdays), *summer* 1.30 p.m. – 6.30 p.m. *winter* 1.30 p.m. – 4.30 p.m.

☕🍴 Cafés in Worcester

🍺 Inns in Upper and Lower Broadheath

🗺 Ordnance Survey 1:50,000 series, no 150

🅿 On Oldbury Road

🐟 To reach the starting place of the walk from Worcester, cross the Severn along the A44. Beyond the roundabout keep on the A44 but almost immediately turn right, down Henwick Road. Go over the level crossing. After ½ mile turn left along Oldbury Road. (Nameplate may be missing but there is a sign 'Worcester College of Higher Education'.) Park and start the walk by the Copper Tops Inn.

Cross the road; an unsignposted bridleway starts by a white house. Go through a field gate (marked Ambrose Farm) and along the farm vehicle track. The wide way soon swings right and becomes a green way that goes over a brook and through a field gate. Walk by the Georgian-looking farmhouse.

By barns take care not to go along the drive (marked 'Private Road') but through a green metal hunting gate. Continue by the left-hand edge of the pasture to a field gate leading to arable lands.

The right of way bears slightly left through the gate to a junction of farm tracks. Walk ahead alongside large oak trees. By a water well (danger sign) swing right towards a cottage. Beyond the gate keep on the drive to the B4204. Turn left and cross the road. Turn off the B4204 after about 200 yards along a tarmac bridleway on the right alongside cottages. Proceed through a metal bridle gate by a cattle grid and go down an avenue of conker chestnut trees.

After ¼ mile the hard way swings 90° right; we turn 90° left through a metal field gate. Stay by the hedge until it turns, then keep ahead to soon pick up the line of another hedge on your left side. Cross over a lane and continue on the same heading to the B4204 at Lower Broadheath.

Turn right, then left at the Bell Inn. (There is another hostelry — The Drop Inn.) Just beyond the inn, on the other side of the road is an expanse of green commonland. Cut directly across the grass, aiming towards a tall single poplar tree. Keep on this heading to a lane at Upper Broadheath. Continue to the left. Along this way is Elgar's Cottage, surrounded by a garden where old English flowers bloom.

After lingering in this peaceful place, take the signposted bridleway nearby. A gentle rise and there is a fine view of Elgar's beloved hills. The bridleway twists this way and that but is clear past Oldbury Farm where you join the farm drive. This leads to Oldbury Road where we began this ramble.

72

A WOODLAND NATURE RESERVE

WALK 23

1½ or 5 miles (2.5 or 8 km)

In the heart of some lovely Worcestershire is Ravenhills, a nature reserve administered by the county's Nature Conservation Trust. The trust hopes to receive a modest amount as a donation towards the expenses of maintaining the woodlands and I am sure it will not be disappointed. When I visited this lovely place even the refreshments were available on trust that folks would put the correct money on the plate!

Today, so much of the countryside as we know it is being destroyed. There is the encroachment of towns and motorways; modern farming methods often destroy hedgerows which are complete minor worlds of nature; chemicals in agriculture destroy plant species (for example poppies which were once so prevalent) and so on. It is therefore of great importance that there are oases of countryside where 'nature rules OK'!

Ravenhills Wood is privately owned and covers about 50 acres. It was thought to have been part of an extensive wooded area which once linked the Royal Forest of Malvern Chase and the Wyre Forest (which is still extensively wooded today). The reserve is partly a working forest and partly wild areas virtually untouched by man. There are also water regions where you will no doubt see wildfowl come and go at will.

Children are encouraged to visit the Discovery Centre where information is given on what to look for. Examples of evidence of animal activity will be displayed now and then and you can also state what you have discovered! It will always repay you to stand and stare from time to time on the nature trails. Explanation of the orange and blue trails can be obtained from the Discovery Centre. The 'orange' is just under ½ mile; the 'blue' is said to be slightly more arduous, sometimes wetter, and longer — about 1½ miles.

The spirit of Ravenhills is epitomized in this motto in the Discovery Centre:

> Long live nature
> Admire it
> Enjoy it
> Care for it
> Understand it
> Manage it
> Protect it
> So man can survive

73

Ravenhills Woodland Reserve, Alfrick (8 miles west of Worcester off A44), is open every day 10.00 a.m. to dusk. *Admission* donations are welcome (suggested 50p adult, 20p children).

Cold refreshments obtainable at the reserve

Inns in Alfrick and near Ravenhills

Ordnance Survey 1:50,000 series, no 150

Street parking Alfrick, car park at Ravenhills

The longer walk starts at the little village of Alfrick. A glance at your Ordnance Survey map will show the light green shading surrounding the village indicating these are orchard lands. Journey here in the springtime and the apple blossom is most pretty.

The tower of the church of Alfrick (St Mary Magdalene) is shingled (wood tiled) and has a sundial bearing the words 'On this moment hangs eternity'. The Normans have left their mark in the building. From the far corner of the churchyard a signposted field path crosses under electricity wires to a stile on the far side of a large field. On a lane turn right then left at the junction. A few twists and turns later we reach Ravenhills Reserve. After your

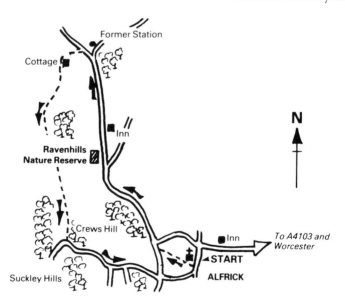

visit, turn left on the lane and climb the hill past the country inn. This climb continues to where a railway once ran. Opposite the 'station' go along a vehicle track signed as a bridleway then continue past a cottage. We come to a high meadow and keep by the right-hand hedge to the far corner.

Now walk on the fringe of beautiful woods and you may well see gems of orchids here and there — rare and delicate blooms. The way marked bridleway is along the ridge of the rather remote Suckley Hills. Keep on these lovely paths always on much the same heading to reach a vehicle track, then a lane at Crews Hill. Turn left to descend steeply by more orchards; walk straight ahead at road junctions to Alfrick in the vale.

MALVERN HILLS

WALK 24

★

3½ or 4½ miles (5.5 or 7 km)

There are said to be twenty summits of the ridge of the Malvern Hills — up and down twenty times in the course of the nine miles, then having to walk back to the starting place seems to be too much of a marathon route march! This walk takes in the highest point. The Worcestershire Beacon is 1394 feet and we cheat a little as we climb in the car to the Wyche cutting — some distance up the slope!

The beauty of the hills inspired William Langland, a poet of the fourteenth century, to compose his great poem *The vision concerning Piers Plowman:*

>In a summer season, when soft was the sun,
>In rough cloth I robed me, as I a shepherd were,
>In habit like a hermit in his works unholy,
>And through the wide world I went, wonders to hear,
>But on a May morning, on Malvern Hills
>A marvel befel me. . .

Since those days the rounded high uplands have inspired artists, poets and men of music.

The Malvern Hills are of some of the oldest rocks in the land. The stones are multicoloured, showing the presence of many minerals, mica, pink felspar and quartz. The minerals are not dissolved by rain and fissures and the impervious layers result in many wells of pure water.

For years this water has been used for medicinal purposes; on this walk we go near a 'holy well'. The worship of the 'miracle' of a never ending source of water dates from early times. This well is dedicated to St Ann.

It was a Doctor Wall, a scientist specializing in porcelain as well as being a physician, who created the spa of Malvern in the mid eighteenth century. Within a year or so the quiet village below the hills became a popular inland resort. The purity of the water gave rise to the local jest:

>The Malvern water says Dr John Wall,
>Is famed for containing just nothing at all!

There were several hillforts placed by Iron Age men to keep a wary eye on the wild Welsh. The most extensive earthworks are perched on the top of Herefordshire Beacon (1370 feet). From our viewpoint on Worcestershire Beacon you will be able to see distinctly the ditches and ridges of the camp.

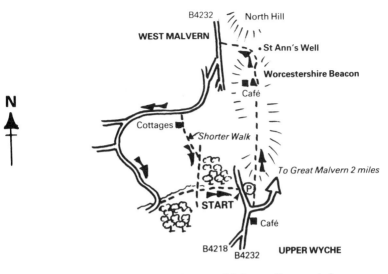

This area was once part of the vast Malvern Forest; it is to our great benefit that the land was not taken from public use at the time of the Enclosure Acts. In 1632 King Charles I decreed that 'none of the forest should be enclosed except His Majesty's one third and that the other two thirds should be left open and free'. Today, the hills are still open and free, so let us go to the high land and enjoy the puffing climb and super views.

Café on summit of Worcestershire Beacon in summer months and at Wyche

Inn at Wyche Cutting

Ordnance Survey 1:50,000 series, no 150

Car park, administered by Malvern Hill Conservators, on B4218 at Wyche

From the junction of the B4218 and the B4232 at Wyche Cutting, take the hard track which wends a winding way uphill. We come to the rocky summit and feast on the marvellous view. This was once a beacon signal station; the poet Macaulay in his poem *Armada* recorded that 'twelve fair counties saw the blaze on Malvern's lonely height'.

There are two plinths on the top — one is the triangulation point; the other bears the biblical text 'The earth is the Lord's and the fullness thereof'. It was erected in 1897 to commemorate the sixtieth year of Victoria's reign and incorporates a toposcope to identify the surrounding hills. Drop down the rocky way to the 'saddle' between two hills. Nearby, is St Ann's Well but we swing left at the directional indicator along a way signposted to 'The Dingle'. Head towards the chequered landscape of Herefordshire.

Walk down the V of the valley towards cottages (Wildmoor and Upper Dingle Cottage). There is now a hard vehicle track to take us to the B4232. Opposite is the Brewers Arms Inn. Turn along the road to the left. Take the turning leading off to the right (Harcourt Road). A few twists and turns and by a de-restriction sign there is a vehicle way to the left if you wish to shorten the route. (At the end of the vehicle track, by the cottages, go through a latch gate then a field gate nearby. Continue with a hedge on your left side for a couple of fields to a stile to a vehicle track. Turn right to rejoin the longer route.)

For this longer way, at the de-restriction sign, stay on the lane to a road junction by a white building (which was once an inn). Turn left along the way signposted to Colwall. Still take the Colwall direction at the next junction. There is a sharp bend after about ½ mile. Go over the railing bridge then, by a wood on the left is a footpath signposted to West Malvern. We are never far from the brook — a well-trodden pathway leads to a vehicle track, where we pick up those folk who have walked the shorter route.

Cross to the vehicle way opposite. Now climbing uphill, go past cottages to a patch of green grass on the left. Here you will see a stile into a hill pasture. Still climbing — no doubt with weary steps — we come to the B4232. The Wyche Cutting is to the right.

CLIMBING SYMOND'S YAT AND VISITING KING ARTHUR'S CAVE

WALK 25

4 miles (6.5 km)

Symond's Yat is a huge rock — the hazards of geology have left this superb natural viewing platform. We look out over a curve of the River Wye; the river bends back on itself to almost complete a circle. The speeding waters have over the centuries cut deep into the rocks to create the spectacular gorge. (Robert Symonds was the High Sheriff for the county of Herefordshire many years ago; Yat is probably Old English for 'gate' or 'pass'.)

The cave we visit is said by local folklore to have been the hiding place of King Arthur's treasure — Merlin the wizard buried the wealth here! Although the cave (discovered in 1870) was excavated about fifty years ago, the only discoveries of note were relics of Stone Age man and skeletons of animals long unknown in Britain, such as the woolly rhino, bear and hyena.

There are two exciting crossings of this lovely river. Early on we tread warily over a 'rope' suspension bridge. You can peer down through the wire grille at your feet to the fast-flowing waters and dream of spotting magnificent salmon! Towards the end of the walk there is a ferry trip at an ancient crossing place of the river.

Seven Sisters Rock is another projecting rock where there are spectacular views of the Wye Gorge. There is another boulder on the opposite bank, Far Hearkening Rock, which sends back sounds. In days past, the gamekeepers picked up the noise of the poachers of deer in this way.

Café with lovely cream ices at Symond's Yat Rock, other cafés by ferry

Inn by the ferry

Ordnance Survey 1:50,000 series, no 162

Car park at Symond's Yat

From the car park walk over the road by the wooden footbridge — this way leads to the rock of Symond's Yat. Retrace your steps to the car park and walk down the road passing under our previous footbridge.

79

Opposite a cottage and arches our way leaves the road by descending to a slightly hidden track on the left (clearly waymarked by yellow arrows). Through a tunnel of branches, the track goes down a shady pathway steeply to the River Wye. Turn left and continue by an hotel. We are now on the route of a railway — probably a slow meandering route and called 'The Elver Express'. This is a wonderful stretch of the river where young people learn the excitement of shooting the Wye's rapids in canoes.

This part of the valley is known as 'The Slaughter'. It is said King Alfred's son, Edward, won a bloody battle here in 910 against the ferocious sounding Dane Eric of the Bloody Axe.

The track continues through lush undergrowth to the Bibblin's Suspension Bridge where we cross the Wye. Safely across, turn left to go by a favourite camping site for Scouts. After ¾ mile, look for an arrow directing us away from the river to the right. A sharp climb now through beechwoods, it is an exciting scramble in places, and then we reach tall cliffs of limestone.

Take a well-earned rest then continue the climb, still following yellow markers. At the summit is the outcrop platform of Seven Sisters Rock; the reward for the climb is a panoramic view of breath-taking beauty. Proceed along the track through the trees to the deep hollow of King Arthur's cave; the flints found here have been dated at 80,000 BC. The path climbs above the cave (still yellow arrows show our way) and soon we can see a quarry.

At a junction of vehicular ways cross to the main 'road', so crossing the route to the quarry. Stay on this main track for only

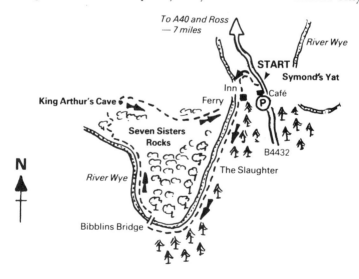

100 yards, then take a footpath arrowed to the left. Beyond a plantation of mainly lofty Corsican pines is an area of young trees about 12 feet tall.

Take care soon — the path divided with no waymarks when I was here. Our way is right. Beyond the small trees we again enter deciduous (leaf shedding) woods and the swift river is heard. We pass more caves — perhaps these are remains of iron-ore mines that were worked before the Romans came. Descend to the right. Watch for the signposted track to take a couple of sharp turns off the main route.

At the river and the rapids we turn left and soon go through an attractive cottage garden. Cross the river by the ferry to the inn; a weary climb now along our outward route to Symond's Yat car park.

TO LUDLOW — FOR FOSSILS AND A NORMAN CASTLE

WALK 26

5½ miles (9 km)

The rocks in the vicinity of Ludlow have a fascinating assortment of fossils which can reveal facets of life millions of years ago. In the youth hostel by the medieval Ludford Bridge, there is a fine display of 'finds' and hammers to chip away at rocks can be hired.

Ludlow is situated on the River Teme — the name is from the old British derivation 'dark river' and is the same root as many other rivers such as the Thames, Tame, Tamar and Tavy.

There is a magnificent castle protected by a wide sweep of the river and steep cliffs. It was in 1095 that Roger de Montgomerie decided this would make an ideal site. Its subsequent use was as a bastion against the wild tribes from Wales.

The unfolding of the story of our land took a twist at Ludlow. Arthur, the eldest son of Henry VII, was born in 1486 — the year after the Tudors won the throne at Bosworth Field (see Bosworth, walk 6). He was in delicate health and was only 16 when he died at Ludlow Castle in 1502. He had been married to Catherine of Aragon for only five months. Who knows what would have been the course of history had Arthur succeeded to the monarchy rather than his brother Henry who was to become the flamboyant and legendary Henry VIII.

 Ludlow Castle is open daily from April to September. In the summer months there are performances of Shakespeare's plays by a distinguished professional company in the castle grounds

 Cafés in Ludlow

 Inns in Ludlow

 Ordnance Survey 1:50,000 series, no 137

 Castle square, Ludlow

 Youth Hostel in Ludford

Cross over the bridge which spans the river Teme, and go along the A49. We go by the popular youth hostel then continue along the main road for about ½ mile.

At Mabbitts Horn, leave the road and go along the drive. Take the left fork near the house. Keep on the track to climb a stile, then proceed at the edge of an arable field. Through a metal gate we walk along a farm track. After a few hundred yards do not go ahead through a gateway (no gate) but go through the nearby wide metal gate.

The farm track immediately bears left — a sunken farm track through a quarry. The sunken track leads to a metal gate, then continues by a cottage (keep just on your right) and a Dutch barn. Through a metal gate we reach woodlands and there are several forest roads. Keep ahead (not the way climbing on your right side). The forest road descends to a quarry and a woodlander's cottage.

Keeping on much the same heading, we soon accompany a brook meandering through Mary Knoll Valley. We are now deep in Mortimer Forest — part of 8,400 acres of Forestry Commission land. Fallow deer roam here, as they have done since Saxon times.

The way the foresters go bears sharp left over a brook. We leave the main track here and take the wide green path on the right. We soon climb beyond the trees to pass through a metal gate. Continue climbing through the oaks and silver birches on a narrower track now. We emerge from the trees and go over rough pastureland — glorious views over the treetops can be seen from this lofty spot.

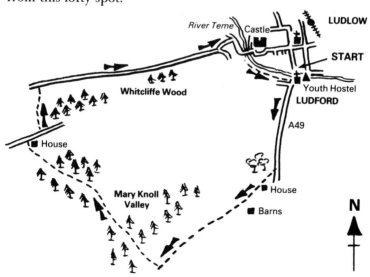

83

Through a metal gate, walk alongside a garden and house to a road. Turn right for a few yards then take a track through a barrier on the left. The way divides at once; take the right fork. Cross a forest 'road' and keep on the same heading to the edge of a wood. We go through a wicket gate to a pasture. A steep descent and we reach a lane. Turn right onto a quiet lane now near the plantations of Whitcliffe Wood. After 1½ miles bear left on a twisting lane, to the ancient bridge below the castle. Either cross the river back to the town or there is a nice riverside path to Ludford Bridge and the youth hostel.

OFFA AND HIS DYKE

WALK 27

6½ miles (10.5 km)

Offa came to power after a civil war amongst the Anglo Saxons in the ancient English kingdom of Mercia in 757, and was to reign a scattered kingdom for 39 years. His western boundary nudged the lands of the wild Welsh — the exact line was ill-defined. To mark and police the frontier King Offa constructed the remarkable and celebrated dyke which stretches never far from the present boundary of Wales from the mouth of the River Wye to the hills above the River Dee; thus it was not built for offensive but defensive purposes.

The dyke was thought to have been made between 778 and 796. In places it is still clearly in the form of an earth embankment and ditch which goes up hill and down dale. Offa, on other stretches of the boundary, used the natural features such as a mountain escarpment or clifftop to define the extent of his land.

Offa's Dyke Path is one of several designated long-distance footpaths in Britain; it is unique in that it follows not a geological feature such as a coastline or ridge of hills but an archaeological one. The entire length of the path is 168 miles. This walk covers a modest few miles but includes one of the best-preserved sections of the dyke. There is a fine youth hostel in a former mill building at Clun, some 3 miles from the starting place of the walk.

Store at Newcastle
Cafés at Clun (3 miles away)

Inn at Newcastle

Ordnance Survey 1:50,000 series, no 137

Quiet roads at Newcastle

Youth Hostel at Clun

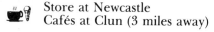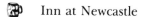 From the centre of the little village of Newcastle leave the B4368 and go along the lane which passes the church dedicated to St John, where there is a novel revolving lych gate. Just after a road junction look for a wire fence and acorn

85

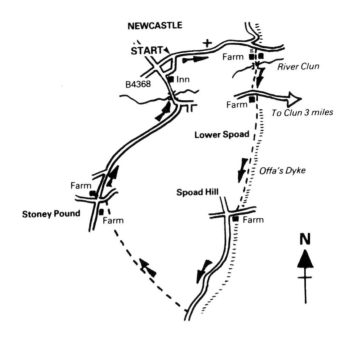

footpath sign on the right. (The acorn sign is the standard symbol used for waymarking on all officially designated long-distance pathways.)

In the pasture we can see the humps where Offa's legions marked out their boundary. Walk down the slope to go through a metal gate into the farmyard at Bryndrinog. Immediately turn left to a footbridge over the river. There is an ancient and quaint farmhouse here.

In the field veer slightly right. Cross over a rivulet — there is an acorn painted on a stepping-stone. Through a metal gate, climb a sheep meadow to a lane by Lower Spoad Farm. A yard or so to the left, we follow the direction through the farmyard, indicated by a pathway signpost. The farmhouse of Lower Spoad has interesting timberwork and dates from medieval times.

Walk by an ancient bus (if you are tired this vehicle will not take you far!), then look for a stile to the left of the farm track. It is a steady climb now with a good section of the dyke; with each step the views become lovelier. We never stray far from the embankment and reach a lane at the height and farm of

Springhill. This lane was once a part of a long ridgeway track which hugged the highland of Clun Forest (these were vast sheep lands and gave their name to a distinctive breed of sheep).

Turn right, then left at the crossroads. The dyke is now clothed in the woodlands to our left. After 1 mile, ignore the waymark sign on the left and stay on the lane for another 100 yards or so. There is a fenced track on the right and this is our way — a clear and breezy route.

At a lane turn left to a crossroads. Here, by the farm at Stoney Pound, we go along the lane to the right. The way drops steeply to the B4368. Proceed to the left to cross the tumbling waters of the River Clun and so back to Newcastle. There is a fine view on entering the village of a steep hill on which was perched an ancient camp.

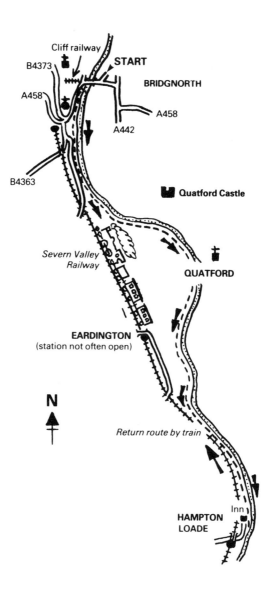

Cliff railway

B4373

START

BRIDGNORTH

A458

A458

A442

B4363

Quatford Castle

Severn Valley Railway

QUATFORD

EARDINGTON
(station not often open)

N

Return route by train

HAMPTON LOADE

Inn

WALK FROM BRIDGNORTH
STEAM TRAIN BACK

WALK 28

★

4½ miles (7 km)

There is something romantic about a steam train — the engines seem to have a personality and a character that the diesels have never acquired. The reward (or perhaps bribe with some youngsters!) on this walk is a homeward journey on the Severn Valley Railway.

The railway is a private company that runs a line from Bridgnorth to Bewdley. For much of the 13 miles it follows the River Severn.

The Severn Valley Railway uses mainly volunteer labour so if you have always wanted to be an engine driver, perhaps this is the place for you. The line was originally opened in 1862 and with the amalgamations then in vogue became part of the Great Western Railway in 1872. The GWR was always considered the peer of all railways with its service and distinctive chocolate and cream livery.

The Bridgnorth to Bewdley line was closed to passenger traffic in 1963 although coal trains used the line to Alveley until 1969. Steam trains started chugging again on the 18th of May 1974. Besides rides by the youngsters of all ages the line has been well used by film and television companies for authentic backgrounds of old steam trains. *God's Wonderful Railway* and *The Thirty-nine Steps* are two films made on the Severn Valley Railway.

The walk starts at Bridgnorth — an historic and unusual town. It is built on two levels. The top town is on a huge cliff; the rest of the place is down below by the banks of the Severn. Between the two towns there is a cliff railway so we will begin and end the ramble on a train!

On the cliff top is a castle wall — the only surviving part of the fortification destroyed during a violent Civil War battle. The wall leans at a crazy angle.

OPEN

The Severn Valley Railway runs from March to the end of October each year (Saturdays and Sundays only outside summer months). *Fares:* from Hampton to Bridgnorth — adults £1.90 (children £1.00)

89

Cafés in Bridgnorth and at Bridgnorth and Hampton stations

Inns in Bridgnorth and Hampton Ferry

Ordnance Survey 1:50,000 series, no 138

Parking at Bridgnorth station

Take the cliff railway to the riverside A458 (22p). Turn right along the main road. Immediately before a garage on the left, go down steps to the footpath by the River Severn. Turn right to follow the waters downstream. We are now following the largest river in the land. The waters rise on Plymlimmon in North Wales and travel 215 miles to join the Bristol Channel.

Climb stiles and soon we have the railway embankment on the right. Take care when the track (still by the bankside) becomes slippery and steep. We then border fields where grain is grown on the rich soils and the river twists far to the left. There is a large mansion hiding behind a wood on the other side of the river. This was the site of Quatford Castle. The house was built in 1830. The wife of the Norman Roger de Montgomery, Adelina, had a stormy voyage across the Channel. Roger vowed he would build a church on the spot where he met Adelina after her safe arrival. So the church on the sandstone rock at Quatford was founded.

After further river paths we come to Lower Forge. Here are chimneys and ruined buildings of the old iron furnaces — some of the places are carved out of the sandstone. It is said by some researchers that these ironworks are even older than those of Ironbridge (see Ironbridge, Walk 30).

The railway is again on an embankment beyond Lower Forge and every so often we have fine views of puffing steam trains. Cross a stream that joins the Severn by going over an ancient cast iron bridge. On the opposite bank there are extensive woodlands — a fine colourful sight in autumn.

So we arrive at Hampton. There is an unusual ferry here; it carries its passengers (mainly anglers) across the fast flowing waters of the Severn by the strength of the current.

A few hundred yards along the lane away from the river, there is the railway station. The line is single track but doubles at the station where you can discover the names and locomotive types being used on the day of your visit. A 'toot-toot', a blow of the guard's whistle and we start the homeward run to Bridgnorth.

YOUTH HOSTELLING ON WENLOCK EDGE

WALK 29

5 miles (8 km)

Scattered throughout England and Wales there are about three hundred youth hostels where, for a modest sum, young people (of all ages!) can find good but simple accommodation. In some, meals are provided but all have facilities for self-catering.

It is fun meeting other youngsters and the hostel buildings range from purpose-built places to humble cottages, mills, castles and manor houses. It is to an historic manor house that we journey for this ramble. Wilderhope Manor is perched on the side of a lonely slope of the Shropshire limestone ridge called Wenlock Edge.

The beauty and tranquillity of Wenlock Edge has inspired novelists, poets and musicians over the ages. The poet A. E. Housman, featured the area in his lyrical poem, *A Shropshire Lad*; these are also the lands of Mary Webb who changed the names of many of the towns and villages in her novels.

Wilderhope Manor is a rambling gabled house dating from the sixteenth century. For years it was rotting and derelict but it was rescued by the generosity of a member of the Cadbury family. A trust fund purchased and restored the manor in 1936 as a tribute to King George V and handed it over to the National Trust with the proviso that it should be used as a youth hostel. There are so many interesting features — secret rooms, winding stairs, maybe a ghost or two and tales of daring escapades; just the place for romantics and historians!

 Wilderhope Manor is open, 2.30 – 5.00 p.m., to the public (other than hostellers) on Wednesday and Saturday afternoons from April to September

 The youth hostel is open most nights except during the winter months (weekends only). It is advisable to book accommodation in advance.

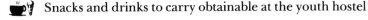 Snacks and drinks to carry obtainable at the youth hostel

Inn on the B4368

91

Ordnance Survey 1:50,000 series, no 137

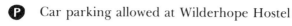 Car parking allowed at Wilderhope Hostel

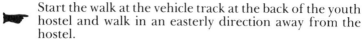 Start the walk at the vehicle track at the back of the youth hostel and walk in an easterly direction away from the hostel.

Have the occasional glance back — the gabled house looks especially haunted and awesome if the wind is scudding black clouds from the west! We are now walking along an ancient road. Go past a farm drive to a T-junction of tracks and turn right. By a cottage the main way swings 90° left. However, we keep straight ahead along a wide green track.

The way divides by a gate with a Forestry Commission notice. We walk to the right along a broad track that goes by Norwegian Christmas trees. Keep on the same path, ignoring others that join. By a steep slope there is a Y-junction. Take the left fork which climbs acutely to a rough pole stile to a pasture. Immediately

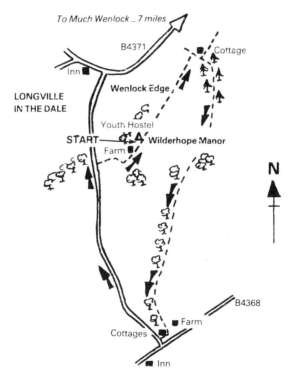

climb another stile beside a tree then turn 90° right to walk alongside a wire fence (on your right side).

You will have a fine view now of the vale with Wilderhope Manor on the next hillside. Stay by the wire, then come to a plantation of tall fir trees (with brambles below). Keep this copse on your left side (walking just in the meadow is best I think). After about 300 yards (at a point where the tall plantation trees change to lower ones) go through a metal gate and into a pasture.

Bear over to the right to the edge of an elongated wood which clothes the hillside. In the very far left-hand corner of the long meadow is a stile to climb. Regain the old heading (wood still on right). On a far horizon to the left is the whale-like hump of Brown Clee Hill. If the visibility is good you may just see the huge white domes of a tracking station.

Go through a metal gate (coppice still on right). There are then several metal gates to negotiate (trees still on right). The way dips downhill — look for a cottage below the far tip of the coppice — as a further landmark a farm is near, just away on your left side.

Through the gate, go by the cottage to another metal gate. Walk over a brook and along the drive to a lane. Our way is to the right, but if you want the inn it is just to the left on the B4368. A steady climb now, keeping on the lane, brings us near the top of Wenlock Edge. You will see the sign of Wilderhope Manor showing the way home along a vehicle drive to the right.

IRONBRIDGE — WHERE THE WORLD'S INDUSTRIAL REVOLUTION BEGAN

WALK 30

5½ miles (9 km)

It was in 1709 that Abraham Darby first smelted iron using coke as a fuel. This breakthrough enabled Britain to become the first industrial nation and the workshop of the world. Because of Darby's unique process we could manufacture the first iron rails, iron boat, iron aqueduct, iron-framed building and iron bridge.

The monument to the first great ironmakers is the bridge which gives the area its name. Ironbridge was a tollbridge to span the River Severn at a spectacular gorge-like valley. It was cast locally and built between 1777 and 1781.

On this walk we go through an area called Coalbrookdale which still retains much of the atmosphere of the momentous times of the makers of the metal which was to widen the horizons of the world.

There are now several museums where one can trace the industrial archaeology. The tollhouse of the ancient bridge (which has now been pensioned off and is only used by foot-travellers) is the starting place of the walk. The little building is now used as an information and exhibition centre but you can still see the tolls levied in days gone by.

Blists Hill Open Air Museum is a 42-acre woodland site on which the ancient industries of the county of Shropshire are being recreated, including a mine as it would have appeared about 1900. Also on show are early transportation systems and near the Severn is the Hay Inclined Plane. The plane is part of the canal system and used to carry canal craft up and down the gorge from the river. It was built in 1793. The Coalbrookdale Museum and Furnace Site contains the ironfounding collection and Abraham Darby's furnace.

OPEN All the museums are open daily from 10.00 a.m. Combined *admission* ticket to all the museums — adults £6.50, children £3.80, (family tickets available)

Cafés and restaurants in Ironbridge; snacks and ices at some of the museum sites

Inns at Ironbridge

94

Ordnance Survey 1:50,000 series, no 127

P Car parks by the Iron Bridge

⚠ Youth Hostel at Ironbridge

From the tollhouse and car park go along the minor road which runs parallel to the Severn— we are chasing the river downstream. When the B4373 is reached bear left along the 'B' road to cross over the river.

Here is the Old Robin Hood Inn. (To the left are the Bedlam Furnaces which were constructed in 1757 and are now being excavated.) However, we go to the right. Keep on the lane for about ½ mile. Just after a white house which fronts immediately onto the road on the right, take a clear footpath (unsignposted) which climbs the bank on the other side of the road.

The track joins a vehicle track and you continue to a road and turn left to Blists Hill Museum. Opposite the entrance to the museum (other side of the road) you will see the gated drive marked Lees House Farm. Follow the drive along the curving way to the house. By the garden gate swing left to walk by the brick barn to a railing stile leading to a pasture where friendly horses graze!

Continue to climb; there is a step stile on the hilltop to a plantation of many types of trees. Another stile leads out of the trees; stay on the same heading. Pass through a gateway (no gate) and continue along a clear path (hedge on the left).

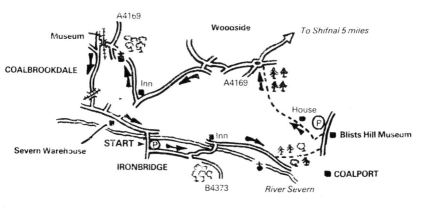

Lees Farm used to be sited at the end of the hedge, but, alas, although it is still marked on maps, the buildings have gone and a modern housing estate creeps over the land. Turn right along the asphalt vehicle drive and keep the extensive Scots pine wood and knoll on your right side.

Stay on the vehicle track (houses on left-side) to a roundabout. Take the second turning, the A4169, signed Ironbridge Gorge. After ¼ mile turn right (Woodside); this is an estate road. After a few hundred yards there is a road called Westbourne. Just beyond take the turning on the left.

The road bears around to the right. Soon take the turning on the right to walk by the White Horse Inn. We come into the woodlands of Church Road where there are fine views over the gorge now, with the massive cooling towers of the power station strangely fitting comfortably into the grand-scale landscape of nature.

At the A4169 cross directly over past the Coalbrookdale Foundries (proudly stating 'Founded 1709'). Above us is a beautifully elaborate clock bearing a date, 1843. Walk under arches to a T-junction — the entrance to the Coalbrookdale Museum showing where the iron revolution all began is to the right, alongside the arches.

Back on the road after your museum visit, walk by the arches; do not go under the arches again, however, but keep ahead along the lane which climbs a wood-clothed hill. This is a quiet and shaded way to the B4378 where you turn left. (On the other side of the road is a riverside picnic site.)

Pass by the Severn Warehouse. Here iron products from Coalbrookdale were stored in the nineteenth century prior to being transferred to barges moored alongside the wharf. The great bridge of iron is ahead.